A Champion's Mindset

Be a Winner Everyday

Faye Donovan

Bohemian Publishing Group LLC

Copyright 2023 Bohemian Publishing Group, LLC. All rights reserved.

No part of this book may be reproduced in any form or by any electronic or mechanical means including information storage and retrieval systems, without permission in writing from the author. The only exception is by a reviewer, who may quote short excerpts in a review.

Although the author and publisher have made every effort to ensure that the information in this book was correct at press time, the author and publisher do not assume and hereby disclaim any liability to any party for any loss, damage, or disruption caused by errors or omissions, whether such errors or omissions result from negligence, accident, or any other cause.

This publication is designed to provide accurate and authoritative information with regard to the subject matter covered. It is sold with the understanding that the publisher is not engaged in rendering professional services. If legal advice or other expert assistance is required, the services of a competent professional should be sought.

The fact that an organization or website is referred to in this work as a citation and/or a potential source of further information does not mean that the author or the publisher endorses the information the organization or website may provide or recommendations it may make.

Please remember that Internet websites listed in this work may have changed or disappeared between when this work was written and when it is read.

Foreword

My voyage into the world of mindfulness didn't begin in the hallowed halls of academia nor in the serene ambiance of a retreat center, but rather in the midst of life's chaos. Moments of overwhelming stress and disconnection beckoned me to the sea of tranquility that mindful practices offered.

Growing up, I was the prototypical overachiever—always striving, always reaching, and inevitably, always burning out. This endless cycle continued into my early career, where the pressures of a fast-paced work life left me feeling like a leaf caught in the current, bereft of any anchor.

It was during one particularly high-tense evening, hunched over my desk littered with projects I no longer felt connected to, that I stumbled upon the concept of mindfulness. A simple, yet profound idea: to be fully present, to experience life in the now without the relentless mental chatter. This idea didn't just pull at me—it tugged with the force of a lifeline thrown to a drowning sailor.

I immersed myself in studies, workshops, and seminars led by leading minds in psychology, spirituality, and personal development. I read voraciously, absorbed teachings from various traditions, and practiced relentlessly. It was a transformative, albeit rocky, expedition from cognitive overload to heart-centered simplicity.

However, the insights I have compiled within these pages aren't just theoretical musings or regurgitated philosophies. Each piece of advice, every guided practice, stems from personal trials and errors, reflections, and revelations.

I met struggle and frustration head-on, particularly when attempting to mesh mindful practices with a demanding schedule. The idea to integrate 'micro-practices' throughout the day sprouted from my need to find balance amidst deadlines, meetings, and the ever-pervasive 'busy trap'.

As an author, my ambition has never been to present myself as the definitive guru of mindfulness. Rather, it's been to serve as a conduit through which these timeless wisdoms could be translated into the vernacular of modern life. A focus which, I hope, you found to be present throughout these pages.

My path eventually led me to step away from the corporate ladder and into the role of a mentor, writer, and speaker. I found immense joy and purpose in guiding individuals and organizations in integrating mindfulness techniques into their bustling routines.

Throughout the years, my work has ranged from guiding solitary retreats to consulting with corporations on creating mindful work environments. One revelation has been incontrovertible: mindfulness is not confined to one's meditation cushion. It is as much about active engagement with our world as it is about internal exploration.

Considering the above, my goal has always been clear: demystify the practices that lead to an awakened life. In doing so, I aimed to bridge the yawning gap between ancient wisdom and the rhythms of contemporary existence—showing that these philosophies are as relevant today as they were millennia ago.

Moreover, I hold firm in the belief that our individual quests for mindfulness can ripple outward, impacting communities and eventually societies. My efforts in penning this text have been fueled by this conviction: that your journey into awakening can be the catalyst for broader change.

In a way, this book is an intimate dialogue, a sharing of life's lessons, a collection of whispers from the heart. It is my sincere hope that you find, within its chapters, something that resonates—a guiding light or a grounding truth, that supports your continued growth.

In bearing my narrative, I trust that you will gather the courage to explore your own story with newfound perspective and invigorated purpose. Remember, enlightened living isn't a concept reserved for the select or the serene—it's a tangible, achievable state for all who choose to pursue it.

Contents

Introduction	1
1. Defining Your Winning Vision	5
2. The Mindset of a Champion	13
3. Cultivating Discipline	21
4. Mastering Motivation	29
5. Overcoming Fear and Doubt	37
6. The Art of Learning from Failure	45
7. The Power of Positivity	53
8. Time Management for Champions	61
9. Building Winning Relationships	69
10. Effective Communication Skills	77
11. Health and Well-Being	85
12. The Balance Beam	95
13. Financial Fitness for Winners	103
14. Mastering the Art of Negotiation	111
15. Leading like a Champion	119

16.	Innovation	127
17.	The Digital Champion	135
18.	Continuous Learning	143
19.	Mindfulness and Presence	151
20.	Recognizing and Celebrating Your Wins	159
21.	Handling Criticism and Feedback	167
22.	Sustainable Success	175
23.	The Ethics of Winning	183
24.	Preparing for the Future	191
Conclusion		199

Introduction

Embarking on the Path to Victory

Picture this: a version of you that's so immersed in the sheer thrill of conquering challenges that every setback becomes a setup for a comeback. You're not just getting through life; you're sculpting it, chiseling away at the excess to reveal a masterpiece underneath. It's not just fantasy. It's a reality that's within your grasp—and this book is your chisel.

Now, imagine having a compass that points you toward your north star, your ultimate vision of triumph. That's what this journey is about. It's not just about crossing the finish line; it's about the grace with which you navigate the track, the resilience with which you rebound from the hurdles, and the tenacity with which you chase after your goals.

The path to victory is as much about the internal triumphs as it is about the external ones. It's about crafting a mindset that sees possibilities where others see barriers. It's about sculpting a life of discipline where routines become the scaffolding for success, motivation fuels your inner fire, and fear and doubt are cast aside like shadows in the noonday sun.

This introduction is not just a welcome message; it's the gentle nudge at your back, the whisper in your ear encouraging you to take that first step, and the assurance that each step you take is a part of building a legacy of victory. And yes, we'll uncover just how to rise from the ashes of failure, because let's be real, the phoenix has nothing on a human ignited with purpose and perspective.

We live in a world where sometimes, it seems like the negative voices shout louder than the cheers of encouragement. That's why cultivating an unshakeable aura of positivity isn't just a nice-to-have; it's as essential as the air we breathe. Positivity isn't meant to shield us from reality's blows—it empowers us to face them with an unbroken spirit.

For the journey to be sustainable, it demands that we manage our time like the limited, precious resource it is. We'll learn that champions aren't just dreamers— they're planners and doers. They wake up each day with priorities that guide their every decision, dodging the snares of procrastination with the agility of a seasoned athlete.

It's not just about individual glory, either. The most awe-inspiring victors are those who elevate others along the way. It's the bonds we forge, the relationships we nurture, and the communities we build that amplify our triumphs. Communication isn't just about making your voice heard—it's about crafting symphonies with your words that move others to action.

The pinnacle of success reaches beyond mere achievement. It extends into how we handle ourselves with grace, fuel our bodies and minds, and create harmony in the chorus of life's endless demands. It's acknowledging that our bodies are the temples housing our winning spirits, which deserve the utmost care through nutrition, fitness, and stress management.

And let's not forget the financial front—a champion's glory is as much in their financial savvy as it is in their ability to lead and inspire. We're not just talking about scrimping and saving here; it's about making strategic, informed decisions that ensure your financial health bolsters your quest for victory.

Speaking of strategy, negotiation is an art form. Imagine mastering the dance of give-and-take with such finesse that every deal you strike is a melody of mutual benefit. This is the heart of winning with ethics—a harmonious blend of integrity, social consciousness, and fair play that cements your legacy.

But the real jackpot is continuous evolution. Staying at the top of your game means being a lifelong learner, always curious, always questioning, and always absorbing. It's about being as flexible in your thinking as you are adamant in your values, ready to adapt with the fluidity of water yet as stable as the rock it molds over time.

Mindfulness is the secret sauce, the ingredient that turns the ordinary into the extraordinary. It's about being fully present in every moment, crystal clear in your intentions, and peaceful in the knowledge that the "now" you're living is as perfect as it is transient.

Let's not cage ourselves within familiar borders, either. Exposure to new cultures, ideas, and environments is the spice that keeps the dish of life piquant. It's the broadening of horizons that turns a narrow path into an open road, paved with the bricks of wisdom gained through experience.

And through it all, there's the celebration of progress—big or small. Recognizing your wins isn't about ego; it's about acknowledging that every step forward deserves applause, even if you're the only one clapping.

Finally, victory isn't merely about withstanding criticism; it's about taking it in stride, refining your approach, and shining brighter with every sharpened edge. It's a continual cycle of receiving, growing, and evolving.

True victory is sustainable, ethical, and prepares you for the future. It's seeing the big picture and understanding how your actions ripple out into the larger pond of life. It's about claiming success in a way that celebrates the individual spirit while embracing the interconnectedness of all things.

Welcome to your path to victory. The celebration of your latent potential, and the flag at the summit of your achievements, all lie within these pages. So take a deep breath, and let's embrace the journey ahead together.

Chapter 1

Defining Your Winning Vision

Leaping from the springboard of our introduction, it's time to laser-focus on creating that image of success that's uniquely yours. Let's face it, a ship without a compass is merely at the mercy of the sea's whims. Envisioning your triumph isn't just daydreaming with your eyes wide open; it's crafting the blueprint for your masterpiece, the rare kind of blueprint that energizes every fiber of your being each morning. Think of it as painting on an expansive canvas where every stroke is a choice, every color a step towards your future, with the picture gradually coming to life as goals take form and purpose, carving out a pathway bloomed with intention and clear direction. But, just as a tightrope walker doesn't glance at their feet, a winning vision demands an upward gaze, fixed on the horizon of possibilities, not the minutiae that often trip us up. In this chapter, we'll dive into the power behind setting goals that resonate with your core and learn how to vividly visualize your climb to the peak, step by exhilarating step, because that's where the magic happens; in the vivid cradle of your mind's eye, where reality is born from the whisper of thought.

The Power of Goal Setting

Imagine standing at the foot of a mountain, gazing at the peak that pierces the vibrant blue sky. You're filled with a mixture of awe and determination. This is the sheer essence of setting a goal: identifying your own personal summit and undertaking the journey to reach it. You align your compass, create a map of the route, stock up your provisions, and step forward with a clear vision in your mind. That's the power of goal setting. It transforms a distant peak into a traveled path and eventual triumph.

Setting goals isn't about hope alone; it's about turning abstract aspirations into tangible plans. It's like planting a seed with intentions. The seed has potential, sure, but it requires soil, water, and sun to grow. Our goals, similarly, need careful nurturing — a mix of strategy, persistence, and the right conditions to flourish. Whether your goal is to run a marathon, write a book, or achieve financial freedom, the foundational step is to set a clear, actionable target.

A goal without a plan can end up like a ship without a rudder, drifting aimlessly or, worse, sinking. Detailed planning — breaking down the journey into smaller, manageable milestones — is central to goal-setting success. Milestones act as checkpoints along the way, providing a sense of achievement and motivation as you conquer each one. It's like a hiker ticking off every landmark while ascending; with each step, the summit inches closer.

Now, let's dig into the significance of specificity. Concrete goals act as a high-definition map of your journey. Instead of 'get fit,' set your sights on 'jog for 30 minutes every day.' Instead of 'save money,' plan 'to save $200 from each paycheck.' The more specific you are, the more likely you are to take the actions required to make it all happen. Specificity turns the invisible into the visible.

Deadlines aren't just for work projects; they're crucial for personal goals too. They create urgency and help prevent procrastination. Attach a timeline to your goals and watch as 'someday' turns into 'by this date.' It suddenly becomes real, doesn't it? And with each beat of the ticking clock, the more driven you feel to act and to act now.

Accountability can amplify the power of your goal setting. Share your aspirations with a trustworthy friend, a mentor, or a coach who can hold you to your commitment. Just like a workout buddy can push you to go the extra mile, an accountability partner can help keep your sights locked on your targets. They can celebrate with you, challenge you, and ensure that you don't lose grip of those dreams.

But what's goal-setting without the belief in the attainability of those goals? Self-efficacy — the belief in one's abilities to meet challenges and achieve objectives — is critical. You have to believe you're capable of crossing that finish line, or it's as good as never starting the race. Cultivate this belief by reflecting on past achievements and recognizing the strength that resides in you. It's always been there.

Goals also guide decision-making and prioritize actions. They are the North Star in the night's sky; every choice you make can be guided by them. When you're faced with a crossroads moment, ask yourself which option aligns with your ultimate goal. It simplifies life's complex decisions and helps keep the distractions at bay.

Adaptability in goal setting is also pivotal. Sometimes life will throw a curveball, and the path to your goal might require a detour. Flexibility doesn't mean abandoning your dream; it means adjusting the sails to accommodate changing winds while keeping your destination firmly within sight. Adaptability equips you with the resourcefulness to overcome unforeseen obstacles.

Goals aren't set in stone. They can evolve as you learn, grow, and discover new passions. Perhaps the most dynamic aspect of goal setting is the ability to refine your goals as you carve your path. It's like sculpting clay — with each day, experience shapes and molds your aspirations into forms that better reflect who you are and who you're becoming.

Visualizing the achievement of your goals adds another layer of potency to the goal-setting process. Imagining the emotions, the environment, and the energy you'll feel when accomplishing your goal can act as a profound motivator. It primes your brain to recognize the resources that will help make your goal a reality.

An invigorating aspect of reaching toward goals is the growth that occurs in the process. Think of it as journeying through a labyrinth; the turns and twists provide lessons and insights that shape you, regardless of whether you reach the center. What you learn through the process of striving to achieve your goals is often just as valuable as the achievement itself.

Intrinsic motivation is the secret fuel behind the power of goal setting. It's the personal satisfaction, curiosity, and passion that drive you. Sure, external rewards can sweeten the deal, but the fire within — that's what will keep you warm on the coldest treks toward your ambitions.

There's also the ripple effect of goal setting. When you strive toward your own goals, you become an inspiration to others. The positive impact spreads and multiplies, encouraging and catalyzing change within your circle of influence. Your quest may originate from personal ambition, but in the end, it can lead to the upliftment of others as well.

Finally, remember that accomplishment is often a mosaic of various attempts. Each step in goal setting, whether forward or backward, is a piece of the larger picture of success. Each piece has its place and its importance. Recognize the incremental victories, and you'll understand that every endeavor, every small win, is part of the extraordinary story you're crafting.

So go ahead, set those goals with audacity, break them down, commit to them, and embolden yourself to reach the heights of your potential. There — just beyond the immediate horizon — lies a version of you that has achieved something beautiful, something worthwhile. Not because it's easy, but precisely because it's worth the climb.

Visualizing Success

Visualizing success isn't just a fluffy concept found in personal development books or the topic of an energizing conference you attended last summer. It's a fundamental tool, one that's been fine-tuned by generations of achievers and innovators who dared to see what doesn't yet exist. You've set your goals high, and now it's time to introduce a method that bridges aspiration and reality.

Imagine a process that not only propels your goals forward but also enriches your mental resilience, enabling you to handle life's ebbs like a seasoned captain in stormy seas. Visualizing success is that powerful engine, transforming nebulous dreams into a palpable future. At its core, visualization is the practice of creating detailed mental imagery of the outcomes you desire, immersing all your senses in the experience of success before it unfolds.

Wouldn't it be transformative to live your victories in high definition before they even materialize? That's the essence of visualization. Picture your success with such intensity that your body can hardly distinguish between imagination and reality. The feel of that handshake sealing the deal, the sound of raucous applause, the sweet taste of a hard-earned triumph. Your brain responds to these vivid rehearsals, priming you for real-life execution.

Dive deeply into the future you're crafting. Visualizing isn't a passive daydream but an active engagement. Draw the blueprints of your success with meticulous attention to detail. Where are you? Who's present? What emotions course through you? The richer the visualization, the more tangible your path becomes. Champion athletes use this trick before they set foot on the field. They've won a thousand times in their minds. Now, so can you.

The beauty of visualization lies in its accessibility; it's a strategy as simple as it is profound. Whether you're waiting for your morning coffee or lying in bed at night, you can whip out this tool and fine-tune your vision. A daily dose of visualization works like compound interest, steadily building the wealth of your potential.

But how do you turn a vision into visceral reality? By consistently reinforcing your vision with positive assertions. Affirmations are the vocal reinforcements that give your imagery its voice. I am capable, I am resilient, I am successful. These statements, repeated with conviction, act as a megaphone to your subconscious, amplifying your visualized goals.

Don't just scratch the surface; immerse yourself in the texture of your anticipated achievements. This is sensory visualization. Can you feel the weight of that diploma in your hands, the brisk morning air as you jog past your previous limits, or the adrenaline surge of your opening night? Engage your senses and watch your dreams gain dimension and color.

Incorporate visualization into your daily routine. Habit bonds actions to outcomes. Bracket your day with morning visualizations of your daily goals and evening reflections on forthcoming milestones. Regularity transforms sporadic practice into an invincible habit.

But it's not just about casting yourself in the lead role of your success saga. Visualization also embraces the potential obstacles you might face. What hurdles could arise on your path? Visualize navigating them with grace and tenacity. This is not to dwell on difficulties but to inoculate yourself against the paralysis of unforeseen challenges.

Perhaps you're grappling with skepticism. Can visualization actually influence reality? It's the underpinning of many leadership styles and the secret weapon of high achievers. By causing physiological and psychological changes that enhance performance, visualization effectively shapes reality. Understand it as mental rehearsal, grooming your neurons for the exact tasks required to win.

As you visualize, cultivate an unshakeable belief in your vision. Doubts may hover like uninvited guests, but your belief is the bouncer at the door of your mind. Trust in the process, allowing the seeds of success to sprout in your steadfast certainty.

Let's not forget that visualization isn't a solitary venture. Share your vision with confidants, mentors, and collaborators. Connect with like-minded peers who can reflect your success in their eyes, adding social reinforcement to your personal practice. Their faith can serve as a mirror, reflecting your potential when you need it most.

Combine visualization with active pursuit. It's like setting a destination in your navigation app; the course appears, but you must drive the car. Visualization equips you with clarity on the destination and emotional incentive, but it's the mindful, consistent actions that truly draw success closer.

There's no better time to start than right now. Close your eyes, take a deep breath, and allow the scene of your triumph to unfurl. In the theatre of your mind, curate an experience so vibrant and real that when you open your eyes, it's as though you're returning from a glimpse of your future. Make visualization a cornerstone of your journey to success, as you draft the blueprint of your destiny with every vibrant mental rehearsal.

As you turn the next page, remember, that visualizing success isn't just about what you see; it's about what you feel, believe, and ultimately do. It's a holistic approach, a confluence of earnest desire, relentless faith, and actionable strategy. Visualize not just the end but every step of the journey, for each stride forward in your mind is a leap towards the reality of living, breathing, and manifesting success.

Chapter 2

The Mindset of a Champion

As we pivot from the clear canvas of goal-setting in Chapter 1, let's now dip into the vibrant hues that paint the essence of a champion's psyche. Picture this: it's not just about the crowning moment of triumph; it's the inner flame that keeps burning through the storm, the silent heartbeat driving relentless progress in the dead of night. You see, champions aren't born in the echo of applause but in the quiet grind when nobody's watching. They've got this steel-clad belief in themselves that doesn't waver at the sight of mountains high or valleys deep. It's an ever-evolving narrative of "I've got this," even when the script of life screams, "You don't!" But hey, let's not get ahead of ourselves—building such ironclad resilience? That's a story for later. For now, let's immerse in the cornerstone of it all: cultivating a mindset that isn't just about wearing the crown; it's about bearing the weight, glory, and responsibility it represents with an unwavering, resolute will to prevail. It's about the steadfast spirit that doesn't just show up; it radiates, turning setbacks into comeback stories that awe and inspire. That, my friends, is where our journey heads next.

Belief in Self: The Foundation of Success

The concept seems straightforward, doesn't it? It's the notion that to excel, to truly harness the power of our potential, we must first believe in our ability to make things happen. The dialogue surrounding self-belief is ubiquitous, but its practice can feel as elusive as a wisp of smoke. Let's dive into the heart of it.

Imagine for a moment - success is a structure you wish to erect. This structure could be a dream career, a personal milestone, or any form of achievement you seek. The strongest material you can use to build isn't tangible; it's the belief you harbor within yourself. Before putting down the metaphorical bricks of hard work, the foundation must be the steadfast certainty that you are able and deserving of constructing that reality.

Now, why is this belief so incredibly vital? It's because self-belief acts as an internal compass that guides you through the maze of life's challenges. When obstacles emerge, as they inevitably will, it's your belief in yourself that will echo in the silence of uncertainty, reminding you that you can navigate through. Without it, it's easy to become lost, disoriented, and eventually stationary.

It's worth noting that self-belief doesn't mean ignoring your limitations. It means recognizing them but also understanding that they don't define your journey's end. It's realizing that skills can be honed, shortcomings can be addressed, and barriers can be breached. It's acknowledging that even though you may not be the best at something today, with persistence and belief, you could be remarkable tomorrow.

Where does such unwavering self-belief stem from? It begins with self-awareness and a truthful assessment of where you stand. This does not imply an overinflated sense of ability, but rather a grounded recognition of your intrinsic worth. It's a realization that your value does not diminish because of someone else's inability to see your worth.

One could argue that belief in self is akin to a self-fulfilling prophecy. Carry within you the conviction that you will succeed, and you set in motion the energy and the mindset that will propel you to take the necessary steps towards that success. Doubt yourself, and you could close the doors to opportunities and self-improvement before they even appear.

But how do we foster such belief? Start by chronicling your past victories, no matter how small. Compile a list of moments when you overcame adversity, when you achieved something you initially thought was out of reach. Allow these memories to serve as tangible evidence that you are capable of success.

Then, surround yourself with affirmations — not just the ones written on sticky notes around your mirror, but also intangible affirmations in the form of supportive relationships and self-improvement literature. These are the nutrients that will feed your fledgling self-belief until it's strong enough to withstand the harshest of doubts.

Keep in mind that belief in self is not a one-time affair. It requires maintenance. Much like a muscle, it needs to be exercised regularly through challenges and reflection. When faced with a new test, remind yourself of the resilience and potential that reside within you. It's a cycle of growth where every challenge surmounted adds a layer of confidence to your belief structure.

Still, maintaining self-belief isn't always going to be a lone endeavor. Sometimes, it takes an external voice to reinforce our inner dialogues. Whether it's a mentor, a peer, or a book that resonates with your spirit, external perspectives can amplify your own, reminding you of the power you possess.

And let's not forget the role of setbacks. Each time you falter, you're presented with a choice — to let your belief waver or to use the experience as a stepping stone to solidify your belief even further. Setbacks are not indicators of failure, but benchmarks for growth. They are the stretches in the journey where belief in self is not merely tested but strengthened.

Moreover, self-belief opens the door to tapping into your full potential. It's a simple equation: the more you believe in your abilities, the more you're willing to take risks and leap for opportunities that might seem daunting to others. It's the daring to advance where others may hesitate that often leads to unprecedented success.

Now, imagine internalizing an unshakable belief in yourself. Imagine the endeavors you could undertake, the heights you could soar to, and the fulfillment that comes with it. It's not a flight of fancy; it's the well-deserved outcome of a steady, inner conviction.

To build this foundation of self-belief, it's important to understand that it's not about never feeling fear or doubt; rather, it's about trusting in your capacity to face them head-on. It's knowing deep down that even when fear and doubt whisper in your ear, the narrative you choose to listen to is the one that says, "I can and I will."

In conclusion, while your path to success will be as unique as your fingerprint, the common denominator across all stories of triumph will always be the belief in self. Embed this foundation firmly beneath your feet, and you're not just stepping towards success; you're leaping towards a future where the possibilities are boundless, and your potential knows no limits.

Building Resilience: Bounce Back from Defeat

Turning the page on belief in ourselves, we delve into resilience, the bedrock that allows champions to spring back after facing defeat. We've all fought tough battles, and sometimes, despite our best efforts, we come up short. It's during these moments, however, where the essence of resilience is both tested and fortified. Let's embark on the subtle art of resilience, a skill that is as critical to success as any strategy or natural talent.

First, understand that resilience isn't ingrained; it's developed. Much like a muscle, it strengthens with practice. Each hiccup in your journey is not a stop sign but a detour sign—indicating a need for a different route, rather than an end to the trip. By accepting that setbacks are a natural part of progression, you've already taken the first step in building your resilience.

It's tempting to let defeat define us—it's often easier to accept failure as a final destination than a temporary station. But here's the twist: your response to failure sets the champions apart from the crowd. Instead of dwelling on what went wrong, focus on what you can do better next time. This mindset is a choice, and choosing growth over compunction is a cornerstone of resilience.

Next, it's essential to maintain perspective. In the grand scheme of life, most defeats are not as catastrophic as they feel in the moment. Ask yourself, "Will this matter in five years?" If the answer is no, then dedicate only the energy necessary to learn and move forward. Keeping a level head about the relative importance of your setback will prevent it from overwhelming you.

Also, don't shy away from examining your defeats closely. It may sting to revisit where things went awry, but scrutinizing your actions is invaluable for growth. Look at your mistakes fearlessly, extract the lessons, and then let them go. Clinging to past errors does not serve you, but learning from them will prepare you for future challenges.

Communication is another vital component of resilience. Instead of isolating yourself in times of defeat, reach out to your support network. Our communities can offer perspectives that reignite our beleaguered spirits and remind us of our worth and capability. A problem shared is a problem halved, and often, just voicing our troubles can lessen their weight.

Moreover, adopt a routine that supports resilience. Whether it's daily journaling, meditation, exercise, or a consistent sleep schedule—establish self-care practices that ground you in your core values and remind you of your goals. A stable foundation in your daily life fosters mental and emotional strength, enabling you to handle defeats with grace.

But let's get physical for a moment. Our physical states impact our mental prowess significantly. Exercise, in particular, boosts resilience by reducing stress and anxiety levels—not to mention, the discipline required to maintain a workout routine is resilience training in itself. Taking care of your body means your mind will be sharper and more prepared to tackle setbacks.

Now, visualization isn't just for victory. Envisioning yourself surmounting obstacles and emerging stronger on the other side can solidify your belief in your ability to bounce back. Reserve some mental space for positive outcomes even in the aftermath of a defeat. Your psyche will thank you for it, and you'll approach future challenges with the confidence of a seasoned survivor, not a fearful freshman.

Alongside positive visuals, it's crucial to remain optimistic but not delusional. Blind optimism can lead to repeated mistakes, whereas hope grounded in reality helps us harness our setbacks as learning opportunities. Reflect on what went wrong, adjust your plans with a dose of realism, and maintain a positive attitude about your ability to improve.

Celebrate your small wins, too. In the face of a significant loss, it's easy to forget the steps of progress along the way. Take time to acknowledge the small victories, no matter how small they seem. These are the breadcrumbs of success, leading you toward your ultimate victory—their signals that you're moving in the right direction, despite any stumbles.

Persistence paired with flexibility is the final piece of the resilience puzzle. Stay dogged in your pursuit of success, but remain nimble enough to adapt to obstacles. Sometimes, the way we've always approached a problem isn't the way forward; be willing to change your methods, try new approaches, and adjust your strategies after a defeat.

One more thing—never underestimate the power of gratitude in building resilience. When you're focused on what's gone awry, it's easy to become blind to the positives in your life. By actively practicing gratitude, you shift focus from what's missing to what's present, from lack to abundance, strengthening your emotional resilience.

Last but certainly not least, remember to be kind to yourself. We can be our own harshest critics, berating ourselves for failures far more than we would ever criticize others. Offer yourself the same compassion that you would a friend. Self-compassion fosters an inner environment where resilience can thrive, nurturing the courage to face defeat and bounce back stronger.

Resilience is more than just a trendy buzzword; it's the hallmark of those who rise to the top. It's not about never falling; it's about how you choose to get up. So, take these steps, weave them into the fabric of your daily life, and watch as you slowly transform setbacks into the building blocks of your greatest achievements.

Chapter 3

Cultivating Discipline

With a crystal-clear vision in mind and a resilient mindset in your toolkit, it's time to roll up your sleeves and get to the core of what turns dreams into reality—discipline. It's the backbone of every success story, the invisible force that keeps you grinding when the spark of motivation flickers. It's not just about willpower; it's about weaving in those daily commitments that align with your goals, finding the fortitude to say 'yes' to progress and 'no' to distractions. Think about it: you've got a reservoir of untapped potential, and all it takes is consistency—like that steady drip of water that can, over time, wear away stone. Discipline isn't shackling—it's liberating! It's crafting those non-negotiables that become as essential as breathing and knowing that each day, you're building a staircase to the stars with your actions. So, ready to transform those 'somedays' into 'today'? It's about setting the stage for excellence through the power and predictability of routine—carving out the winds of habit that'll sail your ship, even when the currents of life seem aimless. Let's dive into the marrow of what makes champions—cultivating discipline—where sweat, grit, and the relentless pursuit of your best self come together to author a story worth telling.

Daily Habits of a Winner

It's like the secret sauce, isn't it? The small, repeated actions that build the staircase to unparalleled success. But what are these habits and how do they carve the path for winners? Let's delve in and line them up so you can start incorporating them into your routine. After all, if you want to walk the winner's path, it's about time to lace up your shoes and start stepping in rhythm to a champion's beat.

First off, winners are early risers. They relish the quiet that comes with dawn. This slice of the day offers uninterrupted time for thinking, planning, and setting the tone. While others are hitting snooze, winners are up seizing the opportunity to get ahead before the rest of the world wakes up.

Let's talk about mindset - it's paramount. Winners infuse their morning with positivity. They often begin with gratitude or a positive affirmation, framing their mind for the day. They aren't just hoping for a good day; they're purposefully crafting it from the moment they wake.

Nourishment – it's not about what you eat, though that's critical. Winners feed their minds with enriching content. Whether it's reading, listening to a podcast, or meditating, they're consuming content that elevates their thought process and prepares them for the day's challenges.

Planning is where thought transforms into action. Winners take time each morning to review their goals and the tasks at hand. They understand the power of intention and prioritize what is necessary to move closer to their vision of success.

But it's not all mental and strategic. Physical health is a key habit. Regular exercise gets the blood flowing and sharpens focus. Whether it's a full workout, a brisk walk, or a series of stretches, winners listen to their bodies and give them the movement needed to maintain peak performance.

Winners also understand the importance of connection. They reach out to mentors, colleagues, and friends to foster relationships that are built on trust and mutual growth. A simple 'good morning' text or a quick check-in call can strengthen bonds and open doors to opportunities.

Discipline is their middle name. They don't dilly-dally or procrastinate when it comes to irksome tasks. Winners tackle the hard stuff first, often adhering to the "eat that frog" philosophy — doing the least desirable task early so it's not looming over them all day.

Throughout the day, winners are hyper-aware of time. They recognize that time is non-renewable and manage it meticulously. They employ techniques such as time-blocking and avoid the rabbit hole of social media and other distractions.

Quality over quantity - winners are focused on doing their best work rather than just staying busy. They're relentless about eliminating unnecessary tasks and are always asking, "Is this moving me closer to my goals?" If not, it's scrapped or delegated.

Another critical habit is reflection. At the end of the day, winners take time to reflect on what they've accomplished, what they've learned, and how they can improve. It's a pattern of continual growth and self-improvement that sets them apart.

Everyone has moments of doubt or frustration, but winners have a way of flipping the script. They use these moments as fuel to push harder and to find solutions, rather than as excuses to give up. Their resilience is not innate; it's built by habitually responding to adversity with toughness and tenacity.

Winners also know the value of shutting down. They have a wind-down routine that helps them transition from work to rest. It might include reading, time with family, or planning for the next day, but the intent is clear: rest is not a break from being a winner; it's part of the winning formula.

We can't talk about daily habits without touching on the importance of sleep. Winners prioritize it because they respect the recovery and clarity that a good night's rest brings. They understand that to perform at their best, their brain and body need to recharge.

The key takeaway here is consistency. Winners don't dabble in these habits; they live by them. Their daily routine might be rigorous, but it's also what elevates them. Every day, they build upon the previous one, cementing the habits that drive them towards their goals.

Lastly, winners are adaptable. They adjust their habits as needed because they understand that life is an evolving journey. If something isn't serving their highest purpose, they are quick to recalibrate and set a new course. It's not about sticking to habits just for the sake of it; it's about maintaining habits that serve their ever-growing vision of success.

So, as you integrate these habits into your life, remember it's the daily commitment that matters. It's about showing up for yourself, day in and day out, with the same dedication that defines winners. Follow these habits, tweak them to fit your life, and watch how they can transform your potential into palpable success. Forge ahead, stay consistent, and you too will start to embody the daily habits of a winner.

The Role of Routine in Achieving Excellence

As we flip the page from exploring discipline, we land squarely on the role of routine in cultivating a life of excellence. It's no secret that the most successful individuals attribute a part of their success to their unwavering dedication to routine. But let's dive deeper into why routine can be the scaffolding upon which a champion's habits are built.

Consistency is the heartbeat of routine. Every time you commit to a particular schedule or set of actions, you're creating a rhythm for your life. This rhythm, believe it or not, is your ally in mastering your craft and in transforming those wild ambitions into tangible realities. It's not enough to have sporadic bursts of effort; excellence demands constancy.

Now, let's tackle a common misconception: routines are inflexible. On the contrary, the beauty of a well-structured routine is that it allows for flexibility within order. When you know what needs to be done and when you can maneuver around life's unexpected hurdles and still stay on track. This is agility within structure, and it's critical in the pursuit of excellence.

Think about the compounded effect of daily habits over time. Small actions, when repeated consistently, can lead to enormous change. The accumulation of these tiny victories is what builds into a wave of success. A routine centered around your goals acts as a compass, always pointing you in the direction of your desired destination.

Detaching from short-term outcomes is easier too when you're rooted in routine. Your focus shifts from immediate results to the process itself. By honoring your daily commitments, you're securing your long-term vision. Excellence, therefore, becomes a byproduct of your steadfast dedication to your routine.

But be warned, the path of routine is not absent of monotony. The grind is real, and it's not always glamorous. Here's where your mindset shifts the game—embracing the mundane as part of your unique journey towards achievement. Remember, the most exquisite diamonds are formed under relentless, repetitive pressure.

Routine also reinforces self-discipline. You become the master of your impulses rather than a servant to them. Each time you choose your routine over a fleeting desire, you strengthen the muscle of self-control. This inner fortitude is priceless in the arena of excellence.

Mental resilience goes hand in hand with a robust routine. When you endure through the sameness, you're building a mental toughness that can withstand the ebbs and flows of life. It preps you for the unexpected, ensuring that your performance is less likely to waver amidst adversity.

Let's not forget the role routines play in mitigating stress. When you have a game plan for each day, decision fatigue is lessened. You won't be plagued by the chaos of the unanticipated; instead, you'll have a reassuring blueprint—a calming force when the storms hit.

An excellent routine is also your silent mentor; it teaches you about yourself. You'll discover when you're most productive, what energizes you, and what drains you. This self-knowledge empowers you to craft a personalized routine that aligns with your inner workings, further maximizing your potential.

There's also a unique sort of confidence that comes from a routine. When you're showing up for yourself day after day, you're instilling a deep trust within. You begin to believe in your capability to execute tasks, overcome obstacles, and push past boundaries. This self-trust is a crucial element in the formula of excellence.

Integration of rest and rejuvenation in your routine mustn't be overlooked. Excellence isn't a never-ending marathon. It's about sustainable productivity which includes time to recover. Structured downtime in your routine guarantees you're operating at peak performance when it counts.

Moreover, routines are signs of respect for your ambitions. When you designate time each day towards your vision, you're honoring your goals. This respect translates into a more profound commitment to the cause, fortifying your resolve in moments of doubt.

For those unsure about how to start, the trick lies in beginning small. Initiate a routine with a few essential elements that align with your vision of excellence. Then, iterate and expand as you become comfortable. Gradual changes ensure sustainability and prevent the sense of overwhelm that can derail the best of intentions.

In conclusion, the role of routine in achieving excellence cannot be overstated. It's a powerful tool that, when wielded with intention and respect, becomes a beacon guiding you through the fog of daily distractions towards the shores of your greatest potential. Embrace routine, let it shape you, and watch as it crafts you into a paragon of excellence.

Chapter 4

Mastering Motivation

After laying the groundwork of discipline, it's crucial to keep the flame of drive kindled within you. Imagine motivation as the fuel for your journey to success; it's what propels you forward when the road gets bumpy. This chapter dives into understanding your deep-rooted 'why'—that intrinsic motivator which is pivotal to maintaining momentum. It's your personal siren call to action, the internal compass that directs your sails towards meaningful goals. But here's the catch - motivation isn't a constant; it wanes like the phases of the moon. Fear not, for we will explore strategies to rejuvenate that zeal and keep that fire burning, even amidst the tempest of life's challenges. As you turn each page, you'll discover how to harness the kind of enduring motivation that not just sparks action but fuels a life-long pursuit of excellence. Prepare to unlock the master key to perpetual propulsion on your odyssey to greatness.

Finding Your 'Why'

As we delve into the essence of motivation, there's a powerful starting line that often goes unnoticed, yet it's pivotal for long-term success. This is about finding your 'why' – the core reason that fuels your aspirations and keeps you tethered to your goals when storms hit. It's that burning passion or purpose that drives you to push through obstacles and pursue excellence, no matter the challenges.

Understanding your 'why' is a transformative experience. It goes beyond the surface level of wanting to achieve something; it's the profound purpose that aligns with your values and gives meaning to your actions. When you find your 'why', every step you take has more significance, every goal gains clarity, and resilience becomes part of your DNA.

You may wonder, how does one find their 'why'? It begins with introspection—digging deep into your personal story, dreams, and experiences. Ask yourself what makes you come alive, what causes or endeavors you are genuinely passionate about, and what legacy you wish to leave behind.

Finding your 'why' is not about what you do—it's about who you are and why you wake up in the morning. It's that invisible force that pulls you towards action even when you're tempted to give in to complacency or despair. Your 'why' leads you to moments of pure exhilaration as you're doing what feels inherently right for you. It's different for everyone, and it's uniquely yours to discover and embrace.

This journey is not without its struggles. There will be times when your 'why' may feel clouded by external pressures or internal doubts. It's during these moments that your 'why' turns into your North Star, guiding you back to your true path and re-igniting the passion that can sometimes wane under the weight of routine or adversity.

Reflect upon your life's most fulfilling achievements—what made them so rewarding? Often, they are tied to deeper purposes, such as connecting with others, personal growth, or contributing to a cause greater than yourself. Your 'why' often lives within these moments of fulfillment.

Remember, finding your 'why' isn't a one-time event; it's a continuous process. As you evolve, so will your 'why'. Life's twists and turns may shift your perspective and priorities, prompting you to refine or even redefine your 'why' over time. And that's perfectly okay.

To effectively find and articulate your 'why', start by writing down what you're passionate about and what you believe your purpose is. Then test it—see if it resonates with your innermost self and if it motivates you to move forward. Talk about it with trusted friends or mentors. Sometimes, the feedback from others can help sharpen your focus, offering insights that align your 'why' with your life's path.

When your 'why' is clear, it propels you through the process of setting and achieving goals. It becomes the foundation upon which you can build a winning vision, from visualizing success to mastering the mindset of a champion. With a rock-solid 'why', the discipline, habits, and routines we'll talk about all fall into place with greater ease and purpose.

Let's consider a meaningful example: Think about athletes who rise at dawn for years, committing to grueling training schedules. It's their 'why' that gets them out of bed each morning—the vision of standing on the podium, the inner drive to excel and push the limits of what's possible, and the dream of inspiring others through their dedication and drive. That's the power of a compelling 'why'.

But this isn't exclusive to athletes. Every one of us has the potential to tap into the wellspring of motivation that is our individual 'why'. It's the flame that fuels not only sportspersons but entrepreneurs, artists, teachers, and anyone who aims for greatness in their field and life.

Don't expect your 'why' to shout its presence. It often whispers, brushing up against the mundane, asking to be noticed. Listen carefully, nurture it, and let it guide you through the ups and downs of your journey towards success. It's one thing to set off on a path, but quite another to know why you're on that path and where it's leading you.

Finding your 'why' doesn't promise an easy road—in fact, it may demand more from you because it matters more. But it's a promise to yourself that the journey and its fruits will be worth the sweat, the sacrifices, and the time invested. It ensures that when you look back, you'll see a trail blazed with purpose, passion, and profound satisfaction.

In the upcoming chapters, we'll delve into keeping the motivation fire burning, overcoming fear and doubt, and cultivating discipline—but always remember that the true catalyst for these achievements stems from this chapter. By finding your 'why', you anchor yourself to a potent source of energy that can sustain your will to win. Your 'why' is the heartbeat of your motivation; keep it strong, and watch yourself begin to move mountains.

Keeping the Fire Burning

You've charted your course, laying out beautiful plans and igniting the initial spark of motivation—it's a thrilling beginning. But now comes the real work: keeping that flame alive, ablaze, and resilient against the inevitable winds of challenge and change. Let's dive into the concept of sustainable motivation. This kind lasts beyond the initial excitement and pushes through the tough times.

It's essential to first acknowledge that motivation is not a constant; it varies in intensity with our environment, emotions, and physical state. The secret to maintaining it is not to attempt a continuous peak, but to manage its ebbs and flows effectively. Think of it this way: Your motivation is like a campfire that needs tending. Sometimes it'll be a roaring fire; other times, it'll dwindle to embers that require care to build back up.

How do you tend to your motivational fire? Start by reconnecting with your 'why.' Remind yourself of the reasons you embarked on this journey. These reasons must resonate deeply with you, so much so that they stir emotion and drive action. This might mean setting aside time weekly to reflect on your goals and progress, keeping these contemplations at the forefront of your mind.

Another key strategy in keeping the fire burning is setting up mini-milestones along the path to your larger objectives. When you reach these smaller targets, the sense of accomplishment fuels your desire to push forward. Reward yourself for these smaller victories—each one is a step on the staircase to your grand vision.

Remember, the environment you're in feeds your fire. Surround yourself with individuals who also seek to better themselves, those who view life as an arena for improvement and joy. Their energy can serve to reignite yours when it falters, and vice versa. It's a mutually beneficial ecosystem of encouragement and inspiration.

Do you understand the power of visualization? It's about seeing the flame of your motivation burn bright in your mind's eye. Practice this regularly; picture yourself overcoming obstacles, reaching goals, and enjoying the process. This mental imagery can be incredibly persuasive in propelling you forward when times get tough.

It's also about finding balance—integrating your work toward goals with rest and recovery. Even the mightiest fire can't burn bright eternally without the occasional addition of fresh logs and time to rebuild energy. Incorporate leisure and downtime into your routine to refresh your mind and spirit.

Let's not forget the language you use on yourself—it can fan the flames or pour water over them. Adopt a positive inner dialogue that nurtures your motivation rather than undermines it. When you catch yourself slipping into negative self-talk, consciously redirect those thoughts towards constructive, motivating affirmations.

A tool often overlooked in maintaining motivation is mindfulness. When you're fully present, you're able to savor the journey toward your goals. This presence can make each step more meaningful and enjoyable, thus keeping your motivation burning steadily.

It's equally crucial to remain adaptable. Sometimes the wind will change direction, and your fire will shift. If you're too rigid in your methods, the flame might go out. Be willing to try new approaches to maintaining motivation. See each shift not as a setback, but as a natural part of the journey, an invitation to learn and grow.

Don't shy away from challenges. They are the very tests that, once overcome, add logs of confidence and resilience to your fire. Remember, the most intense fires often forge the strongest metals. View each challenge as an opportunity to be stronger and more motivated than before.

Nurturing your passion plays a big part too. Align your goals with things you're passionate about. When your work resonates with your interests, it's easier to keep the motivational fire burning bright because your tasks don't just feel like obligations—they're extensions of your passions.

Get into the habit of documenting your journey. Keep a journal or blog about your experiences, your highs, and lows. Writing about your progress can serve as an excellent reminder of how far you've come and can reignite your drive when you read back on it.

Commitment is your fire's best friend. If you've ever witnessed a fire slowly die, you know it requires constant attention. Similarly, your goals require a commitment that doesn't waver. This unyielding dedication, even amidst distractions, keeps the embers of motivation glowing.

Finally, remember to stay humble and keep learning. A fire doesn't grow from a single source of fuel; it needs variety, just like your strategies for staying motivated. Seek out new knowledge, skills, and experiences to continually feed your motivational fire.

By applying these strategies, you're not just tending to your motivational fire; you're turning it into an enduring beacon that guides you through the darkest nights and into the brilliance of your full potential. Keep the fire alive; nurture it, and let it illuminate the path to your ultimate vision of success.

Chapter 5

Overcoming Fear and Doubt

Emerging from the energizing focus on motivation, it's now time to tackle the twin hurdles that often stand between us and our goals: fear and doubt. Like uninvited guests, they creep into our minds, whispering words of uncertainty that can freeze us in our tracks. Picture this: each time fear clutches at your heart, you've got an opportunity to turn it around. Imagine harnessing that adrenaline not as a signal to retreat but as a surge of power propelling you forward. You aren't alone in this; everyone faces this junction of jitters, but now it's your turn to meet those doubts with a steely gaze and a knowing smile. By breaking down the walls of fear and silencing the inner skeptic, you'll discover the boundless courage that lies within. Remember, a life devoid of challenges isn't what we're aiming for—it's the strength to face them head-on that we're after here. Today is as good a day as any to rise above the whispers of doubt, to capitalize on fear as the contrast that makes courage shine. So let's move, with each step reminding ourselves: where there's a will to win, there's a way past fear.

Courage in the Face of Uncertainty

With the right mindset, the enigmatic fog of the unknown can be met not with fear, but with courage and anticipation for the unraveled gifts it holds. In the journey of striving for greatness, uncertainty is not just a lurking shadow; it's a constant companion. The only way to move forward is to greet it with courage.

Courage doesn't mean you aren't afraid. In fact, it presupposes the existence of fear and doubt yet chooses to move regardless. Courage is about decision—taking calculated risks, and leaping into the unknown because remaining stagnant is an even larger threat to progress. It's about making friends with discomfort, because often, that's where you'll find the next level of your personal and professional growth.

Every winner has confronted moments of uncertainty—times when the outcome was beyond the scope of their control, and the path ahead was shrouded. Embracing these moments, not with reckless abandon, but with a confident stride, is what sets champions apart. As such, courage becomes the fuel for transcending barriers and turning the tide in one's favor even when the odds seem insurmountable.

Many believe that courage is innate, a trait reserved for the bold and the fearless. But courage is, in fact, a habit. It's a muscle that gets stronger with use. By intentionally placing yourself in situations where you're not quite comfortable, you gradually become immune to the paralysis that fear can induce. This doesn't mean you won't feel the fear—it just means it won't steer your life.

When faced with a decision where the future is a blur, courage asks you to garner your past victories for confidence. It reminds you to bring forth the memory of every challenge you've ever overcome and to know that you're capable of handling just as much, if not more, going forward. The work you've done in deciphering your 'why,' perfecting your habits, and embracing positivity, all play a role in building up the fortitude required to wade through uncertainty with courage.

Uncertainty often bears the gift of innovation. It's under the blanket of the unknown that the most creative solutions are born. When the usual paths are blocked or nonexistent, the courageous mind begins to consider possibilities previously unexplored. It dares to think in new directions to innovate beyond conventional limits, and therein lies the opportunity for extraordinary success. Winning isn't about always knowing the way; it's about forging a new one when the map ends.

Within uncertainty, you'll also find the space for humility and learning. No champion has ever risen without the foundational understanding that there is always more to learn. The moment you resign to the fact that uncertainty will always be part of the equation, you open yourself up to the vast wealth of knowledge and experience that comes from stepping into the unknown, ready and willing to learn whatever lessons it has to offer.

What's more, embracing uncertainty is a testament to your belief in yourself. It's a bold assertion that whatever comes, you trust in your abilities, your preparation, and your resilience. Courage doesn't ice out fear but coexists with it, allowing your belief in self to dictate your actions, not the whispers of doubt that accompany the unpredictable roads ahead.

It's also important to remember that you're not alone. Behind every triumphant individual lies a collective of past influences, supporters, mentors, and peers. They too have faced their own uncertainties and survived. Reaching out, sharing anxieties, and seeking guidance isn't a sign of weakness but a tactical move of someone with the courage to seek all avenues of strength.

Even when circumstances are unclear, goals can provide a beacon of light. They act as anchors, keeping you oriented and pushing forward even when the storm rages. Having a clear understanding of your long-term objectives enables you to retain perspective amidst the fog of uncertainty. Each small step taken is a movement towards something greater, a testimony to the courage within that won't allow trepidation to dictate your journey.

So, when you find yourself standing on the precipice of the unknown, remember that courage is about perspective. View each encounter with uncertainty not as a threat, but as an opening for immense personal growth and an opportunity for achievements that resonate with depth and meaning. It's the opportunity to exemplify the qualities of a champion, to rise and flourish in the face of the undetermined.

And as you move forward, it's critical to recognize courage in action. It could be the decision to pivot in your career, to start a new venture, or to stand up for something you believe in despite popular opinion. Courage comes in various forms and recognizes no uniform. Still, it's always marked by action—an outward movement against the grain of fear and complacency.

Therefore, cultivate courage. Practice it daily in small decisions so when the mammoth ones come knocking, you're ready and unwavering. Reward yourself for the moments you choose to act courageously, reinforcing the positive behavior and embedding the habit deeper within your character. With each courageous act, you're writing the narrative of a winner, one who faces the unknown not with trepidation, but with undying spirit and resolve.

In your march towards success, remember that uncertainty is merely the shadow cast by new horizons. When approached with courage, it gives way to the warmth of new beginnings and the triumphs that await. The path to victory is rarely a straight line, and it's courage in the face of uncertainty that allows you to chart a course through uncharted territories with confidence and grace.

So, hold your head high and your vision clear as the tide of change and uncertainty tries to sway your course. With courage as your compass, you will navigate through the unpredictability with the heart of a champion, ready for whatever lies ahead, unwritten in the stars, waiting for your audacious heart to discover.

Silencing the Inner Critic

Silencing the Inner Critic is a critical step in journeying towards success. Let's face it: everyone has that little voice inside their head, the one that loves to point out flaws and question every move. It can be relentless, but it need not be unbeatable. Taming this internal saboteur is all about strategies, and it's high time we've equipped ourselves with the tools to dial down its volume.

Imagine the inner critic as an overzealous coach who doesn't know when to take a break. Yes, it sometimes pushes you to do better, but it also burns you out, sours your victories, and keeps the spotlight on your slip-ups. The first step to silencing it? Acknowledge it. You can't fight a shadow, but once you shine a light upon it and name the voices of doubt and self-criticism, you've taken the first step towards diminishing its power.

Now, recognize that the inner critic isn't the truth-teller it pretends to be. Often, it's reliving outdated stories from our past - experiences that shaped our belief systems but aren't indicative of our current capabilities or worth. So, question its narratives. When it whispers that you're not good enough, ask, "Is that truly the case, or is this a relic of an old fear?" Replace the critic's bleak forecasts with evidence of your past successes and strengths.

Self-compassion is your ally here. Treat yourself with the same kindness you would offer a friend in your shoes. When the critic goes on a tirade, pause and reflect on how you'd console a loved one. You'd likely encourage and support them, wouldn't you? Extend that same courtesy to yourself. Self-compassion isn't self-indulgence; it's a vital component of resilience.

Another powerful technique is to externalize the critic. Give it a name or imagine it as a separate entity. By doing so, you create psychological distance, which makes it easier to detach from its pessimistic assessments. When 'Debbie Downer' or 'Negative Ned' starts yammering on, you can consciously decide to turn the volume down or change the channel to a more uplifting station in your mind.

Mindfulness is another key practice in muting the inner critic. By staying present, you can notice when the critic is looming, observe its patterns without getting entangled in them, and let the thoughts pass like clouds in a breezy sky. This disengagement prevents you from spiraling down the vortex of self-critique, keeping your feet planted firmly on the ground of reality.

Putting pen to paper can be a transformative exercise. Write down what the inner critic says, then respond to it as you would in a dialogue. This technique helps you clarify the irrational or exaggerated nature of self-critical thoughts. It can empower you to craft a more balanced, realistic view of yourself.

Let's not forget the importance of a supportive network. Surround yourself with people who uplift you. The individuals you spend time with can either amplify your inner critic or help you silence it. Share your self-doubts with trusted friends or mentors, and often you'll find that they're quick to provide perspective that can drown out the harsh internal dialogue.

Of course, action is a powerful silencer. The inner critic thrives on inaction - the more you ruminate, the louder it gets. But when you're in motion, taking tangible steps towards your goals, the critic has less room to maneuver. It's busy watching you prove it wrong, one accomplished task at a time.

Gratitude can shift your focus away from the critic's negative bias. Make it a habit to acknowledge the things you're grateful for each day. This practice can recalibrate your mindset, shining a spotlight on the positives and shrinking the shadow of criticism.

Tied closely to gratitude is the act of celebrating your wins, no matter how small. Did you tackle a tough project at work? Give yourself credit. Did you stick to your exercise routine? That's a victory. These acknowledgments starve the inner critic of its power, replacing self-doubt with well-earned confidence.

And don't underestimate the power of physical well-being. Regular exercise, adequate sleep, and a nutritious diet contribute to overall mental health, which in turn can bolster your defenses against the inner critic's assaults. When you're physically feeling your best, your mind is better equipped to combat negativity.

Continue to educate yourself on the mind's intricacies. Understanding why you may be prone to self-criticism can unravel the threads that tie you to unhelpful thoughts. Books, workshops, and even therapy can provide insights and tools for breaking the cycle of self-criticism.

Persistence is key. Silencing the inner critic isn't a one-and-done endeavor; it's a continuous practice. Just like building muscle or mastering a skill, quieting the inner critic requires repetition and dedication. Celebrate the moments of silence and learn from the times when it sneaks back in.

In summary, silencing the inner critic is an essential but attainable challenge on the path to personal excellence. By acknowledging its presence, practicing self-compassion, staying mindful, taking action, cultivating gratitude and positivity, surrounding yourself with support, and maintaining physical well-being, you can turn the volume down on self-doubt and amplify your potential for success.

Chapter 6

The Art of Learning from Failure

Think back on the last time you faced a setback—did it stifle you, or did it spur you on to dig a little deeper? Truth is, every winner has their share of losses. But it's what they do next that truly defines their grit. In this journey of transformation, where we've already laid the groundwork for vision, mindset, discipline, motivation, and overcoming fear, we now shift our attention to failure and its silver lining. The real game-changer isn't the misstep; it's the mastery of the bounce back—the resilience to extract wisdom from the wreckage. Embracing failure isn't about glorifying defeat; it's about mining it like the richest ores, uncovering invaluable insights that propel us forward. This chapter isn't a detour; it's a vital stretch of the path where the ground feels unstable, but the lessons are rock solid. Let's roll up our sleeves and build the metaphysical muscle to not just endure failure but to study it, understand it, and make it one of our most profound teachers. As we delve into the art of reassembling our pieces stronger and wiser, we're not just patching up; we're reconstructing a more resilient self, poised for the wins awaiting us beyond this chapter.

Embracing Setbacks as Opportunities

Embracing Setbacks as Opportunities isn't just a lofty idea; it's an actionable approach that transforms the hurdles into springboards for growth. Look around. Every growth story is sprinkled with failures. Setbacks, as much as they pinch, hold the soil that can nourish the seeds of your potential. Let's start there – with that fact itself.

Setbacks often come unannounced, leaving a pang of disappointment, a blow to our ego. At that moment, our vision seems hazed by the dust of defeat. But the true art of learning from failure isn't just about getting back on your feet. It's about analyzing the fall, the misstep, and the reason behind the stumble. It's about gathering insights from the ground up.

Think about it. There's a raw honesty in our moments of failure, a clarity that can often be more enlightening than the chorus of praise. Challenges are the universe's way of asking, "How much do you want this?" Embrace that question. Each setback carries with it a lesson—maybe it's a flaw in your strategy, a gap in your knowledge, or a test of your desire.

We live in a culture that celebrates end results. But what if we pivoted and paid homage to the process, including the obstacles? Every hurdle you encounter is a chance to refine your approach. It's as though life is giving you feedback—and feedback, even when it's tough, is a guide to betterment. Seeing setbacks as opportunities means you are signing up for a course in wisdom, taught by experience itself.

Consider the lives of the greats; they aren't fairy tales. They're epics riddled with adversities, and yet they chose to use each of these instances as a stepping stone. When you hit that bump on the road, take a moment to reflect and then align your focus on the tools you need to overcome it.

Reflect on what this setback taught you about your endurance, passion, and determination.

There's a misconception that strength is shown by an unbroken chain of successes, but the truth is, strength is often best demonstrated by one's response to setbacks. It's in the choice to stay resilient. To build resilience, you must allow the reality of the setback to sink in, accept it, and make peace with it. That's when you can truly move beyond it.

How you talk to yourself during these times is crucial. Swap the narrative of self-pity with one of empowerment. Tell yourself, "This isn't the end. It's a detour, an alternative route to where I'm headed." Confidence is not fixed; it's fueled by the belief that every experience, good or bad, equips you with more artillery for your journey ahead.

Now, think scalability. A setback in one area can open doors in another. It broadens your understanding and, sometimes, redirects you to a path with a view you never anticipated but can appreciate. It's the pivot that can lead to innovation. Obstacles often force us to think differently, to get creative, to be resourceful—it's the soil where the seed of ingenuity sprouts.

Don't just passively go through the motions of recovery. Actively seek out the silver linings and embrace them. Be proactive—hunt down the lessons. Like a miner sifting for gold, you have to process a lot of rubble before you find the glints of progress.

It's also about keeping your eyes on the horizon. Your goals don't become any less attainable because of a misstep. Maybe the journey to them just became richer and filled with more wisdom. Every great adventurer knows detours often lead to the most magnificent discoveries. Don't let fear of repeated failure keep you from pressing forward.

And as you process setbacks, remember you are not alone. Share your experiences with others. Openness can lead to unexpected support, advice, and camaraderie. The path to victory is seldom a solo trek. Lean on your network; often, they can provide perspective or help you navigate the rough terrain.

Most importantly, infuse these moments with positivity. Instead of berating yourself, spend that energy planning your bounce-back. Infuse humor where you can. It may sound counterintuitive, but a laugh amidst the chaos can be the sound of resilience—a clear signal that you're not yet defeated.

Each time you find yourself in the throes of setbacks, remember—they are not full stops; they're commas. They represent a pause, a breath in the narrative of your journey, not the conclusion. These pauses are valuable, giving you time to recalibrate and adjust your sails to the changing winds.

In the end, it's about using these experiences to fuel your growth. Each setback you've faced molds you more into the champion you're striving to become. It's about not just going through the motions, but growing through them.

Indeed, embracing setbacks as opportunities is at the heart of every champion's saga. It speaks to the core of transformation: the journey from what you once were to what you are becoming. And as you continue to write your own epic tale, let each challenge you face remind you that within you lies the power to convert obstacles into the bridges that lead to victory.

The Growth Mindset

The Growth Mindset is precisely the thread that interlaces through failures and success, creating a tapestry of endless opportunity for personal expansion and excellence. Heading into this concept, it's critical to understand that failure isn't the finale; it's often the spark that ignites a deeper journey into our capabilities. This realization opens up a door to a world where challenges aren't obstacles but signposts pointing us toward growth.

Imagine your brain as a muscle, one that can be strengthened and developed through use and challenge. The growth mindset thrives on this premise. It doesn't dodge difficulty; instead, it dives into the deep end of the learning pool every single time, looking to swim stronger, faster, and with more skill. It's about believing that most basic abilities can be developed through dedication and hard work—brains and talent are just the starting point.

With a growth mindset, feedback isn't about who you are; it's about where you can go. You start seeing criticism as valuable information, a sort of compass that guides you to better your skills and strategies. This is how embracing the journey of continuous learning becomes an exhilarating way to live. It's no longer about proving you're smart or talented. It's about improving, evolving, and thriving.

Individuals with a growth mindset look around and see others not as competitors, but as potential teachers. They aren't threatened by other people's successes; they are inspired. Such an outlook propels them to listen, adapt, and incorporate new philosophies and methodologies into their own repertoire. They celebrate their peers' victories as they understand that there's plenty of room at the top for everyone willing to climb.

This mindset doesn't mean you'll be spared from the pains of disappointment. On the contrary, when the tough times come knocking, growth-mindset individuals don't wallow in the 'what ifs' or the 'I should have beens,'. They look at what can be learned from the experience. They dissect their disappointments not to assign blame but to build a bridge to better results next time around.

In the quest for greatness, setbacks are seen as temporary and informative rather than damning. You've heard the saying "Fail forward"? That's the growth mindset personified. It recognizes that in the crucible of failure, the heat can either forge something more resilient or melt resolve. Choosing the former makes all the difference.

The growth mindset is also closely connected to the idea of effort as a pathway to mastery. Sure, talent might give someone a head start, but it's the consistent effort that will lead them across the finish line. And it's not just about crossing the finish line but the intention to keep running race after race. It's a long distance run, and each step, each mile, counts toward ultimate expertise.

Now, how does one cultivate this mentality? Start with being open to learning—always. Prioritize learning over seeking approval. Understand that intelligence and talent are points for launch, but where you soar is a matter of choice and effort. Strive for progress, not perfection, as perfection is an unattainable master that can lead to stagnation.

Also, recognize that effort is complex. It's more than just the physical or mental energy you put into something. It's emotional energy, too. It's the practice of maintaining perspective, reigning in our internal dialogue so it serves us rather than hinders us. It's the stamina of the spirit, the mind's toughness, and the body's readiness.

Collaboration, too, is essential for those looking to grow continually. This mindset urges us to seek others who challenge us and stretch our thinking and skills. It's embracing the symbiotic relationship of teaching and being taught, leading and following. In this dance of exchange, every partner brings value to the floor.

Setbacks, they'll happen; it's part of the process. So when they do, process the emotions but don't pitch a tent there. Self-compassion without self-indulgence is key. Be kind to yourself as you would to a friend going through similar challenges. This is how resilience is refined, and as resilience strengthens, so does the quality of perseverance.

Moreover, celebrate the small successes along your path, the mini-milestones that indicate progress. It's not about waiting to ring the bell at the top but about acknowledging each step that propels you upward. Each achievement is like a reinforcement of the belief that improvement and growth are possible and happening.

Setting incremental goals that lead to larger objectives allows us to focus on continuous improvement. The growth mindset applauds the incremental effort; it adores the nitty-gritty of getting a bit better each day. A concrete plan for growth means having a clear direction for the steps ahead while staying flexible enough to adapt as learning occurs.

The interplay between mind and matter also matters here. Embrace holistic health as it's a critical ingredient to maintaining a growth mindset. After all, a sleepy, stressed, poorly nourished brain does not the fertile ground for growth make. Look after your body, and your mind becomes a more vibrant arena for growth.

Finally, lean into lifelong learning. The world is abundant with knowledge and experiences that can shape us into more complete versions of ourselves. The growth mindset never settles; it's unquenchably curious and untiringly inventive. It yearns for what it hasn't yet mastered and goes after it with the zest of a beginner and the focus of a sage.

This, my friends, is the growth mindset: a compass, a cheerleader, and a challenge rolled into one. It's what transforms a momentary defeat into a stepping stone. Every mishap, every misstep, becomes a lesson in the curriculum of life, every day a school of possibility. So foster your growth mindset, and watch as your horizons expand to contain not only what you thought was possible but also what you haven't even dared to dream yet.

Chapter 7

The Power of Positivity

As we turn the page from learning how a champion embraces setbacks, we allow the warm light of positivity to illuminate our path forward. Harnessing a positive outlook can feel like grafting wings onto your spirit; suddenly, every challenge seems surmountable, and the horizon stretches wide with possibilities. Imagine greeting each day not as a relentless grind, but as a canvas for creation, rich with opportunity. Positivity isn't about wearing rose-colored glasses—it's about choosing to see the value in every experience, to weave gratitude into your life's tapestry, and allowing it to propel you toward your grand vision. Consider the undervalued power of a simple smile, or the ripple effect of an affirmative thought; these aren't mere feel-good mantras, but catalysts sparking joy and energy into action. As you nourish your journey with optimism, watch how a shift in perspective can dramatically alter outcomes, opening doors where once there seemed to be walls. This chapter invites you to harness that transformative energy—the kind that turns dreams into plans, and plans into reality—because a heart uplifted by positivity can't help but elevate everything it touches.

Harnessing Optimism

As we pivot into the realm of positivity within this transformative journey, it's crucial to acknowledge the strength that an optimistic outlook can imbue into our lives. Much like a seasoned gardener knows the importance of sunshine, the nurturing beam of optimism can illuminate our path, even when the road ahead seems shrouded in fog. But let's be clear—optimism isn't about donning rose-colored glasses to obscure reality; rather, it empowers us to envision a reality anchored in hope and potential.

First, we untangle optimism from naivety. To harness optimism means to leverage it as a strategy. It is a conscious choice, a deliberate path we take amidst the array of attitudes available to us. Consider optimism as your trusted compass, a guide that keeps you oriented towards growth and progress, even when challenges and setbacks inevitably arise.

Optimism also infuses our mental landscape with resilience. This isn't merely about expecting good things; it's about cultivating a mindset that stands unwavering in the face of adversity. By believing in the possibility of a positive outcome, we cast a light on solutions rather than getting trapped in a quagmire of problems. We become solution-seekers, defined not by our circumstances, but by our responses to them.

The beauty of optimism lies in its infectious nature. Have you ever noticed when someone walks into a room with a genuine smile and a hopeful demeanor, the atmosphere shifts? Optimism has a ripple effect that can inspire those around you, contributing to a collective elevation of spirit and purpose. By carrying optimism within you, you're not just uplifting yourself but also those on the journey with you.

Now, let's get practical. How do you harness optimism on a daily basis? Start with your first thoughts in the morning. Set an intention to look for the good in the day ahead. Your mind is powerful, and steering it towards positive expectations can make a substantial difference in what you attract and notice as your day unfolds.

Perspective is everything. When faced with a challenge, ask yourself, "What can I learn from this?" or "How can this contribute to my growth?" Transforming obstacles into learning experiences is a core principle of optimism. It enables you to move forward with confidence, knowing that each step, whether seemingly forward or backward, is, in fact, progress.

Language, too, is a tool to harness optimism. The words we speak internally and externally shape our reality. By adjusting our language to be more affirmative and encouraging, we reinforce an optimistic outlook. "I can," "I will," and "I am able" become foundational phrases that underpin a resilient and hopeful narrative.

It's also essential to recognize the transitory nature of life. Just as seasons change, so do our circumstances. Optimism grants us the wisdom to know that difficult times are but chapters in a larger story, and with each challenge overcome, our story grows richer and more compelling. This transient perspective fosters a deeper appreciation for the highs and ensures we don't lose hope during the lows.

Surrounding yourself with optimism can amplify its power. Seek out friendships and alliances with those who embody a positive spirit. Much as crops thrive in fertile soil, your optimistic outlook will flourish in an environment sustained by encouragement and hope.

A key aspect of harnessing optimism is to set realistic expectations. While we pursue an optimistic viewpoint, we must also recognize that life is a complex tapestry of experiences. A balanced approach allows us to maintain our optimism while also preparing pragmatically for various scenarios.

Here's something to remember—optimism is not a static state. It requires nurturing and protection, much like a flame in a storm. There will be moments when your positive outlook faces the harsh winds of doubt or fear. In those times, draw upon your practices, your learned perspectives, and your supportive community. Fan the ember of optimism until it burns brightly once again.

We cannot overlook the power of reflection in maintaining an optimistic stance. Regularly looking back on your journey and identifying moments where optimism led to success serves as a reinforcing loop. It confirms the merit in choosing to see the good, even when it wasn't immediately apparent.

And let's address setbacks squarely—they are inevitable. Optimism is not about eliminating setbacks; it's about handling them with grace and grit. Embrace the belief that every downturn carries the seeds of a potential upturn. This doesn't just make you optimistic; it makes you unstoppable.

Lastly, optimism must be shared. Celebrate your wins with a generous heart, uplift others, and communicate your hopeful perspective. Remember, the strength of your positivity can be a beacon for others who may be struggling with their own battles. In sharing our optimism, we create a synergistic effect that can elevate communities and even societies.

By choosing to harness optimism, we don't just better our chances of succeeding; we transform the very quality of our journey. We pave the way not just for a brighter today but for a hopeful tomorrow. Let's carry this effervescent energy forward as we delve into other pillars of positivity, ready to welcome the abundant wisdom each step has to offer.

Gratitude: A Winner's Secret Weapon

It's a bright, fresh morning, much like the new mindset that's waiting to revolutionize your path to success. Gratitude isn't just a warm fuzzy feeling; it's the ace up your sleeve, the silent power that fuels champions from within. Imagine yourself at the top of your game, where victories aren't just moments but a mindset. That's what gratitude can cultivate in your life when wielded with intention.

Let's talk shop about gratitude. It's not just saying "thanks" when something good happens. It's about actively noticing the blessings, big and small, that pepper your everyday life. A winner uses gratitude to shift focus from what's lacking to what's abundant. This mental switch is more than magic; it's a tool that changes your brain, paving roads towards more positivity, resilience, and, yes, even success.

Studies show that people who possess a strong sense of gratitude have a greater capacity to engage with their environment in a meaningful way. Whether you hit a home run today or struck out, there's power in seeking the silver lining. Gratitude turns every outcome into an advantage, an opportunity to grow and learn.

Reflecting with gratitude also enhances your relationships. Ever noticed how much people crave being around a genuinely appreciative person? It's infectious! When you express gratitude, it strengthens your connections, opens doors, and fosters collaborations that could take you to places beyond your individual reach.

And what about those challenging days? Days when pushing through seems tougher than ever? Gratitude isn't just sunshine and rainbows; it's a shield. It creates resilience, allowing you to bounce back from setbacks faster than ever. A grateful mindset reminds you of past triumphs and the support you've received, equipping you with the armor you need to face any battle.

It also amplifies your motivation. A sense of appreciation in your approach to goals helps sustain the fire within. It's easy to push hard when you're feeling good, but gratitude keeps the engine running even during the rough patches. Celebrate the small wins with gratitude, and the big wins will seem far less daunting.

Speaking of motivation, it also hooks directly into your 'why'. Understanding and valuing the reasons behind your goals deepens that drive. Gratitude can remind you of why you started, anchoring you firmly to your core motivations, even when the tides are trying to sweep you away.

Now, to the skeptics who might view gratitude as 'soft' or far from the aggressive pursuit often tied to winning, think again. Gratitude does not negate ambition; it fuels it. It sharpens your edge by keeping you balanced and grounded. You can chase those dreams harder and farther when you regularly acknowledge the journey that's brought you here and the people who've helped you along the way.

And let's talk about mental health. A sound mind is foundational to a winner's trajectory. Gratitude reduces stress, fends off anxiety, and can even improve sleep. When your mind is clear and at peace, your capacity for strategic thinking, creativity, and focus—key aspects of any winning formula—skyrockets.

Perhaps most importantly, gratitude has a unique way of putting fear and doubt in place. It means you're not just hoping for the best; you're also appreciating the road that's leading you there. This kiboshes many of the 'what-ifs' that lurk in the corners of your psyche, clearing the way for bolder, more confident moves.

Let's not forget about the impact of gratitude on your health. Not only does it potentially improve physical well-being by reducing stress-related symptoms, but by acknowledging and appreciating your body's capabilities, you're more likely to nurture it with the care it deserves.

Learning from failure becomes an entire degree easier as well. A grateful approach to setbacks reframes them not as barriers but as stepping stones, essential chapters in your success story. Imagine the energy shift when you're thankful even for the stumbles because you know they're teaching you priceless lessons.

Adopting an attitude of gratitude catches more than just flies with honey; it creates an aura of positive vibes that attracts opportunities. Persons who carry gratitude as a torch seem to light up a room, drawing in intrigue and possibilities like moths to a flame. It's a subtler aspect of networking, but one that can cement your place as a true player in any field.

So, how does one harness the power of gratitude on a practical level? It starts with small, daily acknowledgments. Take a moment each day to jot down what you're grateful for, engage in meditation that centers on appreciation, or simply start your morning by giving thanks. These practices plant the seeds of gratitude that blossom into your winning edge.

In the tapestry of triumph, gratitude is an essential thread that weaves resilience, motivation, clarity, health, and a positive aura into the fabric. It's an insurmountable component that champions grasp tightly, an 'if-not-this, nothing' element in their arsenal of success. As you move forward, let gratitude be the cornerstone of your journey, and watch as the path before you is lit up with potential and promise.

Chapter 8

Time Management for Champions

As we pivot from embracing a positive mindset to transforming our aspirations into concrete results, we delve into the mastery of time—a resource even the greatest champions can't renew. Managing time effectively is the invisible thread that connects every aspect of triumph. Let's face what we've all felt: time can be a slippery opponent, always seeming to duck and weave just out of reach, leaving you gasping for a moment to catch your breath. But, the true champion learns to dance with time, not fight against it. This conscientious tango involves aligning your day-to-day actions with your ultimate goals, slicing through distractions with the precision of a skilled fencer. Think about it—time is really the arena where our vision, discipline, motivation, and learning curve clash and blend into a harmonious symphony of success. Within this chapter, we'll dissect the principles that enable you to seize each day and prioritize your goals meaningfully, ensuring that procrastination finds no refuge in your schedule. It's about crafting a life where every tick of the clock propels you closer to the podium of your dreams.

Prioritizing Your Goals

You've made it this far and you're on fire, ready to take on the world. Let's fan those flames with something critically important in your quest: understanding the hierarchy of your goals. We all have ambitions and dreams that sparkle in the sunlight of our minds. But not all goals are created equal, and figuring out which ones deserve top billing on your to-do list can make the difference between feeling like a hamster on a wheel and a champion crossing the finish line.

Imagine your goals are like a rock band. Some are lead singers, always in the spotlight, and others are backup singers, important but not the main attraction. It's your job to decide who's taking the microphone and who's harmonizing in the background. Everybody can't be a lead singer or you'd just end up with a shouting match. Prioritizing means giving each goal its place in the choir of your life, ensuring a harmonious blend that leads to success.

But how do you sort through the noise and pick out that headlining goal? Start by asking yourself what lights you up, what gets your heart racing with excitement. Your passion is a powerful indicator of where your priorities should lie. And don't forget to consider the implications of each goal. Which ones have the power to be a keystone, to unlock other goals as a side effect of their achievement?

Next, think about urgency. Would achieving a particular goal now create more opportunities in the future? If so, that's a hint that it might need to rise to the top. Sometimes the most pressing goals aren't the most thrilling, but they are essential stepping stones to grander aspirations. A sense of timing is crucial – striking while the iron's hot could mean the difference between a goal achieved and an opportunity lost.

Beyond passion and urgency, there's the scope of your goals. Picture the big, high-impact goals as boulders and the smaller, short-term goals as pebbles. It often makes more sense to move the boulders first, setting the landscape for the pebbles to fit into the cracks with ease. Be cautious, however, not to dismiss the pebbles—sometimes achieving several small goals can create momentum that makes the boulder-sized tasks seem less daunting.

The trick here isn't just knowing which goals to prioritize, but also being honest with yourself about what you're capable of handling at this moment. Sure, we'd all love to multitask our way to success, but spreading yourself too thin is a surefire way to burn out. Concentrate your efforts where they will be most effective, and give yourself the courtesy of focusing on one major goal at a time where possible.

Consider, too, the concept of balance – it's necessary for a champion's mindset. Balance doesn't mean giving equal time to everything; it means giving appropriate time to each goal based on its priority level. Sometimes your personal life will need more attention, other times your professional goals will be at the forefront. The act of balancing is dynamic, and fluid, and requires constant re-evaluation.

Assess your abilities and resources while planning your goals as well. It's great to aim for the stars, but if you're building a spaceship with no fuel, you're not going anywhere. Make sure you have – or can obtain – the necessary skills, knowledge, and support to achieve the goals you set for yourself.

A note on avoidance: don't let the discomfort of challenging goals push them down your list. Stretching beyond your comfort zone is where growth happens. A goal that scares you, that seems just out of reach, is the one that may deserve the most focus. It's in these discomforts that we often find the most profound opportunities for personal development and triumph.

Now, let's talk strategy. It's one thing to prioritize your goals, but another to create a tangible plan to conquer them. Break down those big-ticket items into actionable steps – identify the milestones that will mark your progress. This approach not only makes the journey more manageable but provides you with a roadmap and checkpoints to keep you on track.

Consistency in your approach to priorities is key. You can't change the lineup every day based on whims. Set a course, and unless there's a compelling reason to shift your focus, stick to it. Commitment to your most important goals will keep you from getting sidetracked by lesser ones that might be easier or more comfortable to achieve in the short term.

And remember, part of prioritizing is also about what you choose to leave out. Learn to say 'no' to projects, activities, or even relationships that do not align with your top priorities. Without the distraction of these, you can devote more energy to what truly matters.

An underestimated aspect of prioritizing goals is reflection. Regularly take the time to reflect on your priorities – are they still serving you? Are you closer to where you want to be, or do you need to pivot? Reflecting keeps your goals aligned with your evolving self and the changing world around you.

Lastly, don't forget to be gentle with yourself. Not all priorities pan out as planned, and that's okay. Life is unpredictable, and the ability to adapt your goals to fit new circumstances is not a failure – it's a skill. Recognize your progress in all its forms, not just the crossed-off items on a list.

A structured approach to your goals, with clear priorities, allows you to channel your energy where it counts. You can't do it all at once, but with patience, focus, and determination, you can build a path to success that's paved with the stones of your most meaningful ambitions. Prioritize wisely, my friends, and the symphony of your efforts will crescendo into the masterwork of your life's achievements.

Avoiding the Traps of Procrastination

Avoiding the Traps of Procrastination can often feel like navigating through a minefield of temptation, where every step must be calculated to prevent getting sidetracked. You've been there before, sitting down with the intention of getting to work, only to find yourself succumbing to seemingly harmless distractions. Procrastination isn't a minor inconvenience; it's a formidable opponent in the battle for success, leading to stress, lost productivity, and a sense of guilt that can stifle your champion spirit.

Understanding why we procrastinate is key to overcoming it. At its core, procrastination is often a way to cope with the anxiety and fear surrounding a task. The task might be overwhelming, boring, or may carry the risk of failure which our minds want to avoid. But remember, like any challenge, procrastination can be defeated with the right strategies.

Breaking your work into smaller, manageable tasks can turn a mountain into a series of molehills. Begin by defining the first small step you need to take. It could be as simple as turning on your computer or writing the title of your report. Often, once you take the initial step, the subsequent ones follow with much less resistance.

Set clear, attainable goals for each work session. Instead of aiming to finish a project in one go, aim to complete a specific portion of it. This gives you a sense of achievement and progress, which can serve as motivation to keep going. Pair this with setting a timer, dedicating a 'focused work period' followed by a short break, and you have the Pomodoro Technique - a powerful ally in your fight against the procrastination dragon.

Creating a conducive environment is another important factor. Remove clutter from your workspace, disconnect from social media, and eliminate any distractions that you have control over. Train your focus by maintaining a clean and organized space that signals to your brain, "It's time to get down to business."

Speaking of business, one of the most powerful tools in your arsenal is accountability. Share your goals with someone else or even with a group of people. Being answerable to someone can significantly increase your commitment to the task at hand. This pressure, positive in nature, can elevate you from the sluggish depths of procrastination to the energizing heights of action.

Additionally, attach meaning to your tasks. Find a way to connect even the most mundane job to your larger life goals. Perhaps completing a task could lead to a skill that'll help in a future venture, or maybe getting through a project could set a precedent for your work ethic. When tasks are woven into the bigger picture, they gain significance and value.

It's also wise to be cognizant of your best working time. Some people are morning larks, while others are night owls. Find your peak productivity time and harness it. During these golden hours, you're more likely to overcome procrastination because your energy levels and concentration are at their best.

Another subtle, yet profound strategy is positive self-talk. Replace thoughts like "I have to do this" with "I choose to do this" to empower yourself. This little shift in language can massively transform your mindset from one of obligation to one of autonomy and control over your actions. After all, you're the master of your destiny, not a bystander.

Don't overlook the role of self-compassion in this journey. Instead of beating yourself up for past procrastination, recognize that every moment offers a new opportunity to make different choices. Approach your tasks with a spirit of forgiveness and understand that setbacks can be stepping stones to mastery.

Deal with barriers as they come. If a particular aspect of a task is holding you back, identify it and ask for help if needed. Demystifying a task by learning a new skill or seeking expert advice can make what once seemed daunting entirely doable.

Reinforce your victories with rewards. When you complete a task, celebrate that win, no matter how small. This positive reinforcement strengthens the habit of action and starts to build an internal association between work and reward. It could be a tasty treat, a walk in the park, or time with a favorite book – anything that acknowledges your effort and reinforces your path to victory.

And let's talk about visualization – not just the end result, but the process. Envision yourself working through the tasks easily, imagining your focus and the satisfaction of progress. This mental rehearsal primes your brain for action and makes the real-life enactment of the tasks feel more familiar and less intimidating.

Let's not forget, that procrastination can sometimes signal that you're in the wrong field, or that a task might not just be a priority right now. Reflect upon the importance and relevance of your tasks. If they align with your goals, then they're worth overcoming procrastination for. If not, it might be time to reconsider your commitments.

In sum, overcoming procrastination is about understanding yourself and implementing strategies that align with your personality and lifestyle. It's about being mindful, intentional, and compassionate with yourself as you navigate your way towards becoming a champion of your time. It's about recognizing that you hold the power to beat procrastination, task by task, day by day.

With these tools in hand, you're now ready to take command of your time and take action towards your goals. As you close this chapter and reflect on the insights shared, remember that every moment is ripe with opportunity, and procrastination is simply a hurdle, not a roadblock, on your journey to excellence.

Chapter 9

Building Winning Relationships

As we turn the page on time management strategies, let's dive into the heart of what makes our efforts resonate beyond mere personal achievements—**Building Winning Relationships**. You see, the fabric of success is often woven tightly with the threads of relationships we nurture along the way. This isn't just about rubbing elbows in high-powered networking events; it's about fostering genuine connections that are as much about giving as they are about receiving. It's the kind of synergy you create when you combine the collective strengths of a team, the wisdom offered by a mentor, or the support given by peers who have your back. Effective relationships amplify our victories, not because we can't win alone, but because together, we can win bigger and better. What's the key, you ask? It's cultivating an authenticity in your interactions that makes others see the winner in you, making them want to join forces to create an unbeatable team.

Networking with a Purpose

Networking with a Purpose - the term itself calls to mind a focused, strategic approach to forming connections that are not just about collecting business cards or amassing LinkedIn connections. It's about building relationships that can help you and others grow. And growth, in essence, is at the core of achieving our highest potential.

Let's talk about why networking with a purpose is critical. You see, when we network with intention, we're looking for more than just superficial gain; we're aligning our social interactions with our personal vision and goals. Networking becomes a two-way street where value is given and received, where relationships are nurtured and can eventually blossom into opportunities for mutual success.

Consider this: the relationships you cultivate are like garden plants. Some will sprout quickly, some require patience, but all need consistent care. Similarly, purposeful connections thrive on sincere interest and continual engagement. But how does one begin? Start with clarity about what you aim to achieve. Then, seek out groups and individuals who share similar values or have achieved what you aspire to.

Attending events and social gatherings is just one part of networking. Strike up conversations. Be inquisitive. Ask about others' projects and interests. Listen actively. It's not just about what you can get from these interactions, but what insights and resources you can offer. A powerful network is reciprocal; it's about building trust and supporting one another towards collective success.

Networking with a purpose also means being selective. Time is a non-renewable resource. Invest it in relationships that align with your vision.

It's okay to pass on certain events or connections that don't fit within your scope. This isn't about being elitist; it's about being efficient and intentional with your time and energy.

What about social media? It's an undeniably potent tool for networking. Use platforms to connect with like-minded individuals, join discussion groups, and share your knowledge. Comment thoughtfully on posts that spark your interest, and don't hesitate to reach out with a personalized message to someone whose work or insights resonate with you. Remember to bring value—not just in persona, but online too.

Comfort zones - they're cozy, but they've never been conducive to growth. To network with purpose, you'll need to step out of yours. Initiate conversations, be the first to extend a hand, or make the invite. Challenge yourself to meet new people and engage in different environments. This is where courageous curiosity plays a significant role, and it pays dividends.

Here's something to meditate on: quality over quantity. It's tempting to think a vast network is a strong one, but that's not always the case. Would you rather know many people superficially or have a select few you can truly rely on? Cultivate deep connections with fewer individuals rather than spreading yourself too thin. Depth is a hallmark of purposeful networking.

Technology has given us the superpower to connect across continents and time zones. Leverage this. Build international connections; they can offer diverse perspectives and opportunities that might not be available in your immediate geography. These relationships can sometimes be the catalysts for life-changing experiences or paradigm shifts in your professional journey.

Let's not forget mentorship. As you network, look for potential mentors and also opportunities to mentor others. This exchange of knowledge is invaluable. Mentorship relationships can be instrumental in achieving goals, overcoming challenges, and making pivotal decisions. Network with the foresight of building mentors and becoming one.

As you expand your network, keep an eye on synchronicity. Sometimes, the most random connections can lead to the most profound opportunities. Stay open to the unexpected and embrace the serendipity in networking. Purposeful doesn't have to mean rigid; flexibility can reveal paths and partnerships that rigid planning might miss.

Think about the lasting impact of your connections. Network not just for immediate gain but for potential long-term collaborations. Sometimes, a connection made today may not bear fruit until years later. Nurture these long-term relationships. Stay in touch, offer help, and when the time comes, these seeds may grow into cornerstones of your success.

Avoid transactional networking. It's easily sensed and often off-putting. Aim to build relationships where engagement doesn't end when immediate needs are met. Be genuine in your interactions; approach networking as an ongoing process rather than a one-time task to be ticked off a checklist.

Finally, reflection is key. After every interaction, take time to reflect. Consider what you learned, what you contributed, and how it aligns with your goals. Adjust your strategies as needed. Continuous improvement is the backbone of purposeful networking just as much as it is in any other aspect of personal growth.

In the end, networking with a purpose isn't just a strategic approach to your social interactions—it's an art form of building relationships that support and inspire a symbiotic climb to success. It's embracing the idea that while our dreams and goals are our own, the journey there is a collective one, enriched by the people we choose to include in our story.

Mentorship and Teamwork

Mentorship and Teamwork are not mere buzzwords—they are the scaffolding that supports the architecture of success. Let's talk about the power of mentorship first. Imagine having a guide, someone who's traversed the path you're on and understands the pitfalls and triumphs that lie ahead. This person is not just a teacher but a confidant, a sounding board, and at times, the wind in your sails when the waters get choppy.

Mentorship often begins with a spark—a recognition of something in another person that resonates with your own aspirations. Seeking out a mentor requires bravery, which means admitting you don't have all the answers, and that's perfectly okay. It's a step outside the ego, inviting someone in to challenge and inspire you.

The right mentor can offer invaluable insights because they have one thing you don't—experience. They've felt the sting of failure and the rush of success, and they can help you navigate toward the latter while learning from the former. They provide perspective that can help flatten a learning curve that might otherwise seem insurmountable.

And it's not just about receiving wisdom. The mentor-mentee relationship is reciprocal. It's a dialogue, not a monologue. You bring fresh eyes and new energy that can also invigorate your mentor. It's an exchange where the value flows both ways.

When it comes to teamwork, let's clear the air: no one achieves greatness in isolation. It's a team sport. Your team can be anyone—family, friends, colleagues—who share your vision and support your journey. They're the ones you brainstorm with at midnight and the first you high-five when a plan comes to fruition. They're not just passengers; they're co-pilots.

The synergy of a team produces a collective intelligence that is smarter than any one member. It's like a hive mind that buzzes with ideas, creativity, and problem-solving prowess. A well-oiled team anticipates each other's needs and fills gaps without a second thought.

Trust is the bedrock of effective teamwork. It's what allows each member to take risks, speak openly, and rely on the others. Without trust, the team is just a group of individuals working next to each other, not with each other.

The beauty of teamwork lies in diversity—diversity of thought, experience, and approach. This blend means that when faced with a challenge, you have a rich tapestry of perspectives to draw upon for solutions. It's like having a multimodal GPS guiding you to your destination.

Setting collective goals is as important as setting personal ones. The power of a team aligning behind a shared objective is immense. It creates a unified direction and purpose that propels the entire group forward, with everyone reading from the same map.

Communication within a team can't be overstated. It's the lifeline that keeps the collective heart beating. Misunderstandings and assumptions are the adversaries of progress. Open, consistent dialogue is the antidote.

When challenges arise—and they will—a strong team doesn't dissolve into blame and discord. Instead, it bands together. The members lean on each other, knowing that a setback is just a setup for a comeback if tackled together.

Conflict within a team isn't a death sentence; it's an opportunity for growth. The trick is to handle disagreements with a focus on resolution, rather than victory. It's about finding the best way forward, not proving a point.

Accountability within a team is the glue that holds everything together. When each member takes responsibility for their role and contributions, it fosters an environment of reliability and trust, which is essential for collective success.

Just as a mentor can push and challenge you, so can a team. They are your accountability partners, there to ensure you don't slip into complacency. There's a gentle, yet firm pressure to not let the group down, which can often be the nudge you need to push through barriers.

In conclusion, embracing mentorship and fostering teamwork are transformative strategies. Each has the power to catapult you from the realm of wishing into the exhilarating world of doing and achieving. They are not just parts of your journey; they are the rocket fuel propelling you to your destination. So gather your tribe, find your guide, and arm yourself with the collective brilliance that these relationships offer. Together, you're unstoppable.

Chapter 10

Effective Communication Skills

After building the framework of winning relationships, let's now delve into the linchpin that holds them together: *Effective Communication Skills*. It all starts with honing the fine art of listening—a skill that can catapult you to success. When you truly listen, you're not just waiting for your turn to talk; you're present, picking up on non-verbal cues and understanding the subtext beneath the words. It's a high-octane fuel for empathy and connection which, if you get it right, can transform interactions in both your personal and professional life. And then there's speaking with confidence—something many aspire to but few truly achieve. This isn't about dominating conversations or showcasing your expertise, but rather about speaking with clarity and purpose, ensuring your ideas resonate deeply with your audience. Remember, it can be easy to slip into the comfort of monologues, but your true strength lies in dialogue—engaging, persuading, and rallying those around you with the simple yet profound power of your words. As you flex the muscle of effective communication, every aspect of your life can shift, taking you closer to your peak potential.

Listening to Win

Listening to Win pulsates at the core of effective communication. But before diving headfirst into the depths of this art, let's anchor ourselves into the reality of just how pivotal listening is. Active listening isn't simply about letting the other person speak while you silently tally your grocery list in your mind. It's about fully tuning in, locking onto their words, their intonation, and the dance of non-verbal cues that speak volumes more than words ever could.

Consider listening as the bedrock of understanding, the kind that underpins every meaningful relationship, whether personal or professional. When you listen to win, you're not aiming for victory over the other person, but rather striving for a win-win outcome where understanding shines and relationships flourish. It's the passport to gaining insights. Like any discerning traveler, you'd want to have it stamped with experiences that enrich and empower.

Become conscious of your listening habits. It's seductively easy to slip into passive hearing - a half-hearted engagement where we're partly there but not wholly present. You've got to shelve that approach if you're gunning for greatness. Instead, adopt a laser-focused attentiveness that seeks to grasp not just the words, but the full spectrum of communication. Delve deeper, beyond the superficial, to where true intentions and feelings reside.

Listening with intent allows you to unearth a trove of information—a person's fears, hopes, and dreams. It enables you to empathize, to stand in their shoes and gaze through their lenses. This isn't about being nosy; it's about being genuinely interested in their worldview. And here's the kicker: when people feel understood, they open up more. It kicks down barriers and builds trust, all which are crucial ingredients in the recipe for successful interactions.

There's a gambit some of the most powerful connectors use, and it's called reflective listening. It's mirror talk. It's repeating or paraphrasing what the other person has just said, not parrot-style, but with understanding. This does double duty—validating the other person's feelings and ensuring no vital detail slips through the cracks of misunderstanding.

Question with curiosity. Posing questions doesn't just clarify your comprehension; it shows that you're invested in the conversation. It demonstrates that you're not merely absorbing but also analyzing the information, turning it over in your mind like a gemstone to see all its facets. But here's the hook: your questions must be rooted in genuine curiosity, not as a platform to launch your own agenda.

Let's not skirt around the elephant in the room: distractions. They're as prevalent as the air we breathe. In a world splintered by pings, rings, and digital dings, maintaining undivided attention is a tough nut to crack. But crack it you must. Winning listeners manage their environment—they mute notifications, maintain eye contact, and exude a steady calm that says, "You're the most important thing right now."

Body language talks. It's the subtle symphony that plays along with the spoken word. To listen to win, you've got to tune into these non-verbal sonatas. Sometimes the body shouts what words only whisper. Crossed arms, a hesitant shuffle, or an exuberant gesture—each has its own lexicon that smart listeners decipher.

As you lend your ear authentically, listen not just with the intention to respond, but with the passion to understand. It's not a tennis match where you're primed to lob back a reply the second the ball's in your court. Instead, it's about absorbing, mulling over, and then responding with thoughtfulness that adds depth to the discourse.

Feedback is a listening goldmine. We're often so wrapped up in sharing our perspective that we miss critical insights that could pivot our path to success. When you receive feedback, treat it as a precious metal—analyze its content, its implications, and its veracity. While not all criticism is constructed with golden intentions, the nuggets of truth within can be invaluable.

Avoid interrupting. Nothing slams the door on winning communication quite like interrupting. It signals impatience and disrespect, and frankly, it's conversationally uncouth. Wait your turn, hold your horses, and when the time is ripe, bring your perspective onto the stage with grace and, dare I say, style.

Listen to the silence; it's where omitted details often hide. Spaces between words are not empty voids to rush past but are pregnant pauses that may signal the need for further probing, or perhaps a moment for the other person to gather their thoughts. Respect that calm as part of the conversational rhythm.

Keep an open mind. Biases can distort our listening lens until we hear what's being said through a filter clouded with preconceptions. Shed your assumptions like an old coat in spring and approach every conversation with a freshness that says anything is possible. This is how winning listeners foster connections bursting with creative potential.

Active listening isn't passive agreement. You can be a consummate listener and still hold firm to your convictions. The winning twist is accorded respect to differing views. It's about understanding the contours of another's thoughts without necessarily reshaping your own. Be open to being influenced, but also to wholesomely influence in return.

And finally, know when to wrap it up. Every symphony has a crescendo, a peak where things could not be more potent. Honor that in your dialogues. Bring closure with a concise summary, a heartfelt thank you, or an agreed-upon action step. Train your listening muscles to flex and relax to the rhythm of meaningful exchange. Remember, in the symphony of success, your ability to listen to win plays the sweetest melody.

Speaking with Confidence

Speaking with Confidence ... it's that secret sauce, isn't it? That special something that sets apart the impactful from the unnoticed. But let's dispel a myth right here: confidence in speaking isn't a rare gift bestowed upon a select few; it's an art that can be learned, honed, and mastered. You've learned to set goals, build routines, motivate yourself, and bounce back from setbacks. Now, it's time to voice your vision with authority and conviction.

First, understand that your words carry weight. When you speak, you're not just sharing information; you're transmitting energy, influencing perceptions, and leading emotions. Consider the most memorable speeches in history—they moved hearts because they were delivered with powerful conviction. Your words can do the same in daily interactions, presentations, or crucial conversations.

To speak with poise, begin with a sturdy foundation: your posture. A straight back, square shoulders, and an aligned neck signal to your audience and to yourself, that you're poised and ready. This isn't just about appearances; posture affects your breathing, which in turn impacts the tone, volume, and clarity of your voice. Picture your words flowing from your core, steered by a breath that's both steady and calm.

Nervousness is the nemesis of confidence. So here's a counterintuitive tip: embrace your nerves. Nerves are a sign that you care about what you're saying, and they can be channeled into dynamic energy that propels your speech. Use techniques like visualization to anticipate success, and practice deep breathing or grounding exercises prior to speaking. The jitters won't disappear entirely, but you'll learn to dance with them.

Clarity in your message is paramount. A confident speaker knows what they want to convey and does so with precision. Before you speak, distill your message to its essence. What is the core of what you want to communicate? Can you summarize it in a single sentence? Simplify where you can because simplicity is the soul of eloquence.

Leverage the power of the pause. In our rush to fill silence, we often trip over our words. Pauses are powerful—use them to punctuate your points, breathe, and give your audience time to absorb what you're saying. A well-placed silence often speaks louder than a stream of words.

Your choice of words matters. Vocabulary can elevate an idea or sink it. Opt for words that are precise and vivid, but also accessible. You want to connect with your audience, not alienate them. Cultivate a rich vocabulary, but use it wisely, not to show off but to clarify and enhance your message.

Modulate your voice to keep your listeners engaged. An even, monotone delivery is the quickest way to put your audience to sleep. Instead, vary your pitch and pace to highlight key points and express emotion. A drop in volume can invite listeners in, while a rise can drive home a point with energy.

Practice makes...progress. Rehearse your speeches, pitches, or responses to questions in a variety of contexts—alone, in front of a mirror, with a friend, or recorded on video. Notice patterns in your delivery that you want to change, and work actively on them. Repeated practice builds muscle memory for your voice and your confidence.

Active listening enhances speaking. When you're conversing, don't just wait for your turn to talk. Truly hear what the other person is saying. Engage with their points, ask questions, and show that you value their input. This creates a reciprocal relationship where your confidence encourages openness in others, facilitating richer dialogues.

Own your mistakes. If you trip over a word or lose your train of thought, don't panic. Acknowledge it with grace, and move on. Perfection isn't the goal—connection is. Your audience will relate to and respect your authenticity more than flawlessness. Being comfortable with imperfection actually boosts confidence, since you're no longer in fear of making a mistake.

Storytelling is a confidence carrier. People resonate with stories more than with abstract concepts. Integrate personal anecdotes or relevant stories into your communication. This not only makes your speech more engaging but also provides a narrative structure that's easier for you to deliver naturally and confidently.

Regarding your body language, remember it speaks before you do. Gestures and expressions form part of your message and can enhance your spoken words. Use your hands to emphasize points and your facial expressions to convey your emotions. However, be aware of nervous ticks or repetitive movements that can distract from your message.

Finally, stay curious and continually learn about the art of speaking. There are always new tools, techniques, and styles emerging. Explore them and integrate what resonates with you into your own style. No one ever "finishes" learning to communicate; each conversation is a chance to refine your art.

Embracing and projecting confidence isn't simply a method to influence others; it's a celebration of your inherent worth. When you truly believe in the value of your thoughts and experiences, that belief resonates in your words, enlivens your gestures, and emboldens your voice. Speaking with confidence is, above all, an act of self-respect. It's a declaration that what you have to say matters—and it does. Carry this belief into every interaction, and watch as the world leans in to listen.

Chapter 11

Health and Well-Being
The Champion's Fuel

As we pivot from honing our communication prowess, let's not skip a beat and dive into the very essence that powers our drive—our health and well-being. Think of your body and mind as the high-precision vehicles that will transport you through the twists and turns on the road to success. To maintain peak performance, you can't just fuel up on any run-of-the-mill snacks and stress; you've got to be choosy. It's time to get intentional with the nourishment we give ourselves and the way we recharge. If we're talking about nourishing the body, we're talking about the greens, the grains, the good stuff that makes you feel like you can conquer marathons—even when you're just sprinting through your to-do list. And stress, oh, it can be a sly fox, lurking in the shadows of our busy lives. But don't let it fool you; it's defeatable with the right techniques, making you not just resilient but practically invincible. So let's rally our spirits, tune into our bodies' needs, and gear up to become that unwavering force, the champion who's always ready for what's next, thanks to a foundation of robust health and indispensable well-being.

Nutrition and Fitness for Peak Performance

Nutrition and Fitness for Peak Performance is where the rubber meets the road on the path to victory. Like a well-oiled machine, your body needs optimal fuel and maintenance to operate at its highest capacity. Eating right and staying active isn't just about looking good—it's about feeling powerful, sharp, and ready to tackle each new challenge with gusto. Let's dive into the wellspring of health and vitality that can surge you toward your peak performance.

First up, nutrition isn't just about eating less or more; it's about eating smart. The science is unequivocal in revealing that what you feed your body can dramatically affect your energy levels, mood, cognitive function, and, of course, physical performance. Reflect on what you're putting into your body as if it's premium fuel for a high-performance engine. Imagine every meal as an opportunity to enhance your potential, every snack as a chance to fortify your resolve, and every sip of water as a step towards optimal hydration and concentration.

Speaking of water, let's not overlook hydration. It's key in regulating body temperature, keeping joints lubricated, preventing infections, and delivering nutrients to cells. As simple as it sounds, drinking ample water is a cornerstone of both physical fitness and cognitive acuity. Furthermore, sometimes what we interpret as hunger pangs can actually be our bodies crying out for hydration. Remember: Your brain is around 75% water, so when you're dehydrated, it's like your grey matter is working on fumes.

Now, onto macronutrients—proteins, fats, and carbohydrates. They're the big three that your body needs in large amounts. Protein is like the building block of your muscles and tissues; without it, recovering from workouts and building strength is a challenge. Fats are not the enemy—they're essential for brain health, energy, and cell growth. And carbs? They're your body's preferred energy source. Picking the right type of each—such as lean proteins, healthy fats, and complex carbs—is not about strict restrictions but striking a harmonious balance that fuels your unique body in the best possible way.

Don't forget micronutrients—the vitamins and minerals that are essential in smaller amounts but play an enormous role in energy production, bone health, immunity, and more. When you look at your plate, aim for a rainbow—diverse colors often mean a broad range of nutrients that can help you not just perform well but also protect against chronic diseases.

Moving on from what goes into your body to what you do with it—fitness is the second crucial component of peak performance. Regular exercise strengthens not just your body but your mind as well. It's documented that physical activity boosts endorphins, which can reduce stress and improve mental well-being. A strong body is a resilient body; your physical fitness can carry you through demanding times with grace and agility.

A common misconception is that hours upon hours at the gym or running marathons every other week are required for true fitness. Not so. Consistency beats intensity in the long run. A daily routine that you can stick with raises your heart rate, builds strength, and keeps flexibility in check is invaluable. This could be as simple as a brisk walk, a quick yoga session, or bodyweight exercises. It's about moving daily in ways that uplift and empower you.

Strength training deserves a special shoutout. It's not just for bodybuilders or athletes. Building muscle is vital for everyone. More muscle equals a faster metabolism, better posture, and reduced risk of injury. As we age, we naturally lose muscle mass, so incorporating strength training into your routine isn't just for aesthetics—it's a crucial part of maintaining a functional, capable body throughout your life.

Stamina and endurance are your allies in the marathon of life. Cardiovascular exercise, whether through swimming, cycling, or whatever gets your heart racing, can significantly boost your heart health and overall stamina. It's not just physical endurance that's ramped up but psychological stamina as well, aiding you through extended projects or stressful periods at work or home.

Remember, your body and mind are deeply interconnected. When you're physically active, you're ensuring that rich, oxygenated blood is nourishing your brain. Your cognitive functions—from memory to problem-solving—get a corresponding lift. Exercise is indeed a tool that sharpens the mind as it strengthens the body, making it a non-negotiable for peak performance.

It's crucial to listen to your body and recognize signs of overtraining or malnutrition, which can lead to burnout or injury. Rest and recovery are not lazy indulgences—they're essential components of a balanced fitness routine. Even the most finely tuned athletes require downtime to repair and strengthen themselves.

Moreover, the relationship between your gut and brain is something to heed. The foods you eat can influence your gut microbiome, which in turn can affect mood and mental health. Ensure your diet is rich in fiber, probiotics, and whole foods to foster a gut environment that promotes a happy brain and a balanced mood.

Lastly, be mindful of supplements. They can be valuable in addressing specific deficiencies or providing convenient forms of nutrition. However, don't rely on them to compensate for a poor diet. Whole foods contain a synergistic blend of nutrients that work together to maintain your health. Supplements should complement, not replace, a nutrient-dense diet.

Peak performance isn't achieved by a single sprint or a day's worth of healthy eating; it's the culmination of consistent, mindful choices and actions. Integrating smart nutrition and a well-rounded fitness regimen into your life isn't necessarily easy, but it's undeniably worth it. As you fortify your body, you also galvanize the very spirit that can carry you to the pinnacles of success in every endeavor.

And with that, we've laid the foundation upon which you can build your temple of triumph. As you continue forward, remember that each step taken with intention in the realm of nutrition and fitness is a step towards realizing the potent potential that resides within you. Onwards, towards health, strength, clarity, and beyond—to the peak of your performance.

Stress Management Techniques

Stress Management Techniques lie at the heart of sustaining peak performance and embracing the comprehensive well-being necessary for a champion's journey. It's about more than just shaking off a bad day; it's about developing a toolkit that aligns with our deepest values and visions for success. So, how do we navigate the everyday stressors that come our way? How do we keep our composure when the heat is on? Let's dive into some actionable techniques to manage stress and maintain our winning edge.

The first technique is as foundational as it is powerful: deep breathing. When stress tightens its grip, it's often our breath that becomes shallow and erratic. By intentionally slowing down and deepening our breaths, we tap into our body's natural ability to relax. Try this: inhale slowly for a count of four, hold for a count of seven, then exhale slowly for a count of eight. This isn't just woo-woo talk; it's about activating your parasympathetic nervous system, signaling to your body that it's time to calm down and de-stress.

Did you know that movement can be a potent stress reliever? Yes, regular exercise isn't just for keeping fit; it also helps in busting stress. Whether it's a rigorous session at the gym, a brisk walk in the park, or a dance party in your living room, getting your body moving increases endorphins, our natural mood lifters. Make it a non-negotiable part of your routine, and watch as it provides clarity and reduces the fog of anxiety.

Our thoughts have immense power over our emotions and stress levels. Cognitive restructuring is a technique that involves identifying and challenging stress-inducing thoughts. Does your mind always jump to worst-case scenarios? Are 'what if' questions constantly plaguing you? It's time to reframe those thoughts. Replace the negative with positive, possible solutions. It's not about putting on rose-colored glasses but rather about realistically assessing situations and determining constructive steps forward.

Meditation and mindfulness have gained popularity for a reason. They're not just trendy; they're transformational. Allocating time each day to sit quietly, focus on your breath, and bring your attention to the present moment can significantly reduce stress. It helps in quieting the noise and chaos of our day-to-day lives, bringing a sense of peace and calm that is invaluable in managing stress.

Schedule relaxation into your day. That's right, schedule it. It's as critical as any meeting or deadline. Whether it's a warm bath, reading a book, or lingering over a cup of tea, find what soothes your soul and make time for it. See it as recharging your batteries, giving you renewed energy to tackle your challenges.

A balanced diet plays a more vital role in stress management than you might realize. Those sugar highs and caffeine jolts? They're not doing you any favors in the stress department. Instead, nourish your body with whole foods—think fruits, vegetables, lean proteins, and whole grains. These provide a steady stream of energy that helps keep stress hormones like cortisol in check.

Quality sleep is another non-negotiable for managing stress. We often underestimate the power of a good night's rest, but it's during sleep that our bodies recover and regenerate. So practice good sleep hygiene—keep your room cool, dark, and quiet, establish a relaxing bedtime routine, and aim for 7-9 hours of sleep per night. You'll wake up less stressed and more equipped to handle what comes your way.

Journaling can be a powerful outlet for stress. Writing down your thoughts and feelings helps in processing them instead of allowing them to bubble up inside. It's a form of self-therapy, allowing you to clarify your thoughts and concerns and, quite often, stumble upon solutions you hadn't considered before.

Sometimes, the best stress relief comes from connecting with others. Maintaining a supportive social network isn't just good for your social calendar; it's essential for your mental health. Talking through stressors with friends or family can provide new perspectives, not to mention the immediate comfort of feeling understood and valued.

Time management is a stress management technique in disguise. By effectively managing your time, you can avoid the panic that comes with last-minute rushes. Prioritize tasks, set realistic goals, and break down big projects into manageable chunks. Remember, feeling in control of your time means feeling less controlled by stress.

Practice saying 'no.' Spreading yourself too thin isn't a badge of honor; it's a one-way ticket to Stressville. Understand your limits and protect your time. When you say 'no' to things that overextend you, you say 'yes' to more focus, more energy, and less stress for the things that truly matter.

Listen to music. The sound waves that soothe the savage beast can do wonders for the stressed-out human as well. Whether it's classical music that calms the mind or your favorite rock anthem that pumps you up, music has the power to shift your mood and dissipate stress. Make playlists that resonate with your soul and use them as an auditory escape hatch when needed.

Adopt a hobby or interest outside work. Immerse yourself in activities that have nothing to do with your daily job or responsibilities. This can create a sense of balance and provide a refreshing escape that contributes to reduced stress levels. Whether it's painting, gardening, or learning a new instrument, let this be your sanctuary.

Lastly, remember to practice gratitude. Reflect on what you're thankful for, either verbally or in a gratitude journal. This simple practice can switch the frame from lack and stress to abundance and peace. Over time, it builds resilience against adversity—turning the focus away from stress and towards appreciation for the positives in life.

Armed with these stress management techniques, you're better equipped to face challenges head-on. Lean into them, let them become second nature, and you'll find the balance necessary to achieve not just victory, but a life marked by health, happiness, and enduring success.

Chapter 12

The Balance Beam
Managing Life's Demands

As we step off the platform of health and well-being from our last chapter, let's tiptoe with precision onto the balance beam of life. It's no secret that today's world hurls countless demands our way, leaving us desperately juggling our jobs, relationships, and personal needs. Imagine you're an acrobat, poised and concentrated, maintaining equilibrium on that narrow beam. Each step is deliberate, each movement calculated—because one misstep can send everything tumbling. It's about syncing every slice of your existence, finding that sweet spot between pushing hard and holding back. Sure, we've all felt the twinge of guilt when turning down an invite or duty, yet learning to say 'no' is akin to a deft dismount—it's not about disappointing others; it's about sticking the landing for your own well-being. Balance doesn't mean equal hours in all life's aspects; rather, it's about knowing when to pour energy into a pressing project or when to retreat for some self-care. The goal? To keep advancing without wiping out, to carve out a path that respects both our ambitions and our need for rest. So, as we navigate this beam, let's embrace the wobbles, anticipate the shifts, and cultivate a sense of harmony that doesn't just keep us upright, but propels us forward with determination and grace.

Work-Life Harmony

Work-Life Harmony is a concept that, for a long time, seemed as mythical as a unicorn in the wild. But, as we dig into this crucial aspect of sustainable success, let's recognize that harmony is not about balancing scales with equal weight on both sides. Instead, imagine a symphony where different instruments come together, not always in equal measure, but in a way that creates a captivating harmony. The pursuit of work-life harmony is about creating a life composition where the various elements complement, rather than compete with one another.

Much like a maestro leads an orchestra, you have the ability to conduct the flow of your life. Imagine your career, personal relationships, self-care, and passions as different sections of the orchestra. There will be times when your career needs to take the lead, and others when personal matters need your attention. Striving for harmony means recognizing these dynamics and allowing yourself the flexibility to shift focus as the melodies of your life require.

In the relentless pursuit of success, it's tempting to pour all of your energy into work, leaving little room for anything else. But ask yourself – what's a victory without someone to share it with? What's the point of reaching the top only to find you've sacrificed your health and happiness along the way? The secret is to integrate, not just balance, the various aspects of your life in a way that fuels your overall well-being and success.

Consider the power of presence. When you're at work, be fully there. Give the tasks at hand your undivided attention and your best effort. Then, when it's time for family, friends, or self-care, be just as present. By compartmentalizing your focus, you maximize the quality of your engagement in each area, crafting a tapestry of excellence across all facets of your life.

To cultivate this harmony, let's talk about boundaries – the unsung heroes of mental and emotional well-being. Establishing clear boundaries between work and personal life isn't about keeping a rigid schedule; it's about creating space for each part of your life to thrive. By setting these boundaries, you communicate to yourself and others what's important and when.

Reflection is a tactic often overlooked. Regularly stepping back to assess how your work is affecting your personal life, and vice versa, can provide insights into adjustments you might need. Reflection isn't about judgment; it's about recalibration. By checking in with yourself, you become a proactive architect of your life symphony rather than a passive bystander.

Harmony also flourishes with the power of "no." Learning to say no, whether it's to extra projects, social commitments, or any other potential time thieves, is paramount. It's not about shunning responsibility or opportunities; it's about honoring your capacity and maintaining the quality of your performance in all areas.

Communicate your needs and your vision for work-life harmony with those around you. This isn't a solo journey; your colleagues, family, and friends play supporting roles in your life's composition. By expressing your priorities and sharing your plan for harmony, you enable others to support you and respect the boundaries you've set.

Evaluating your time allocation can reveal much about where your priorities currently lie. If your time doesn't reflect what you claim to value most, then it's time for change. Reassigning your time is a commitment to give weight to all parts of your life that matter, allowing them to flourish and feed back into your overall satisfaction.

Flexibility within your pursuit of harmony is key – life is unpredictable and will throw the occasional curveball your way. Instead of striving for a rigid structure, adopt a flexible mindset that can accommodate the unexpected while still maintaining your focus on your overarching harmony.

Remember the importance of self-care. It's the foundation that supports every other aspect of your life. If you are not at your best, both your work and personal life will suffer. Prioritizing exercise, nutrition, sleep, and relaxation is not selfish – it's essential. Treat these elements as non-negotiable appointments with yourself.

Delegate responsibilities when possible. It's easy to fall into the trap of believing you must do it all, but this is a surefire path to burnout. Delegation allows you to focus on your strengths and gives others the opportunity to shine. Trusting your teammates, both at work and at home, builds mutual respect and a sense of shared purpose.

Re-evaluate and readjust your strategies as your life evolves. What worked for you five years ago might not be suitable today. As you grow in your career, your personal life will also change, and your approach to harmony should reflect these shifts.

Lastly, embrace the concept that perfection is a myth. Work-life harmony is not about creating a perfect equilibrium; it's about making conscious choices that serve your well-being and your ambitions. Accept that there will be imperfections along the way, and that's okay. How you respond and adjust to those imperfections is what shapes your path to success.

By nurturing all spheres of your life, work-life harmony becomes achievable. It allows you to savor the silence between the notes, the moments that are often overlooked but are just as vital to the music of life. With each decision, each boundary set, each no, and each reflection, you're crafting a harmonious life that resonates with success, fulfillment, and joy.

Saying 'No' to Stay on Track

Now, let's shift gears to something that might feel a bit uncomfortable at first, yet it's absolutely critical to staying on track: saying 'no.' This tiny word holds tremendous power. It's what sets boundaries around the life that you've worked so hard to design. It's essential to realize that every time you agree to something that doesn't align with your goals, you're not just saying yes to an activity; you're saying no to your priorities, your dreams, and ultimately, to the championship life you're building.

Imagine you're navigating a maze – each turn you choose either leads you closer to the end or back into confusion. Saying 'no' functions in the same way; it keeps you from wandering down paths that don't lead to your Finish Line. But it's not just about saying 'no' to the big, obvious distractions. It's also about the subtle, seemingly insignificant time-wasters that chip away at your focus and drive.

Next up, you're probably wondering, "How exactly do I say 'no' without ruining relationships or missing out?" It begins with understanding your limits. You're not a superhero – even champions need to recharge and reset. Recognizing your limitations isn't a weakness; it's about knowing your capacity and valuing your time.

It's also vital to assess opportunities based on your goals. If an ask doesn't align with where you're headed, it's taking you off course. Here's a tip:

create a simple decision-making framework. If an opportunity doesn't meet your predetermined criteria, it's an automatic 'no.' It's not about being rude; it's grounded in a commitment to your vision.

But what about FOMO, the fear of missing out? It's natural to worry about passing up what might be a great opportunity. Here's the thing, though – not every 'great' opportunity is great for *you*. When weighing the pros and cons, factor in your long-term gains over short-term satisfaction.

Being tactful is part of the equation as well. You can express your refusal with grace and clarity. It's about the delivery - a simple, "Thank you for thinking of me, but I can't commit to this right now due to other priorities," can go a long way. Be honest and direct, but also kind and respectful.

Consider, too, that 'no' isn't always an outright rejection; sometimes, it's a 'not right now.' Timing is crucial, and certain opportunities might be better suited for later stages in your journey. Don't burn bridges – instead, leave the door open for future collaboration under the right circumstances.

And here's another perspective: saying 'no' can actually lead to more respect from others. People value those who have a clear sense of direction and aren't afraid to stick to it. Setting boundaries can strengthen your reputation as someone who is decisive and stays true to your values.

Remember, you're not alone in this. Many successful individuals have learned the art of saying 'no.' It might start with a bit of discomfort, but as you practice, it becomes part of your winning formula. And let's be clear – 'no' is a complete sentence. You don't have to justify, argue, defend, or explain your decision if you don't want to.

What if saying 'no' backfires? Sometimes, despite your best intentions, your refusal might not be well received. Stand your ground. Your time and energy are precious, and guarding them is not just your right, but your responsibility to the future you're building.

Don't forget to say 'no' to yourself as well. It's not just about external requests – internal distractions can be even more persuasive. Resist the urge to veer off course with activities or habits that don't serve your end goals. This internal discipline is what differentiates good from great, contenders from champions.

Another key aspect is to not let guilt get the best of you. Guilt can make you waver and commit to things out of obligation. Ditch the guilt – you're not obliged to meet everyone's expectations, especially if it's at the cost of your own mission.

Lastly, reflect on the freedom that 'no' brings. There's liberation in choosing your commitments and giving yourself the space to focus without being spread thin. Each 'no' frees you up for that big, resounding 'YES' to your dreams.

In closing, saying 'no' is an act of empowerment. It's a strategic choice that maintains the integrity of your vision and propels you toward your goals. So, flex that 'no' muscle without apology. Your journey to excellence depends on it.

Chapter 13

Financial Fitness for Winners

Stepping into the realm of financial fitness, you'll uncover the secrets to not only surviving but thriving in today's tumultuous economic climate. You've honed your vision, fortified your mindset, and crafted discipline into your daily life – now it's time to tackle one of the most crucial domains of winning: your finances. Think of money management as the ultimate endurance sport. Here, fiscal strength isn't measured by sheer numbers, but by the savvy and strategy with which you handle your resources. Ready to transform your economic outlook? It's about making informed decisions, harnessing the power of compound interest, and cultivating a portfolio that reflects both your goals and your values. Tighten your grip on your budget, lean into the curves of smart investing, and you'll lap the competition on the track to true wealth. Financial freedom isn't just a prize; it's your new baseline, setting you up for a life where you call the shots, and you're always poised for victory.

Budgeting for Success

Budgeting for Success can sound like a heavy, dry topic - let's not kid ourselves. But what if I told you that mastering this could be your key to unlocking realms of potential you never thought possible? It's the framework that supports the grand designs of your life. Whether you're saving up for that dream vacation, aiming to buy your first home, or getting your business off the ground, your budget is the blueprint that lays the foundation.

Think of your finances as a garden. Seek to understand what resources you have available – your income is like rainwater, necessary for growth. Expenditures? Think of them as the various plants in your garden, each requiring a bit of your resources to flourish. A weed here and there isn't the end of the world, but left untended, they can choke out your financial flowers. That's where budgeting comes into play. It helps you allocate your rainwater wisely, ensuring that your financial ecosystem thrives.

Budgeting is planning, aiming, and setting your sights on the future you desire. It's about making conscious decisions with your money, rather than letting it slip anonymously through your fingers like sand. When you create a budget, you're actively choosing to divert funds to your goals – now, that's empowerment.

But where do you start? The first step is understanding your cash flow. Record your income and list down all your expenses. Find out where every dollar goes – yes, even those morning coffee runs. It's all about visibility and getting real with yourself.

Once you've got a handle on what's coming in and going out, set your priorities. Align your spending with your true values. Ask yourself, what matters most? Is it ensuring a comfortable retirement, supporting your family, or perhaps funding your education? Whatever it is, let your budget reflect that.

A crucial part of this financial journey is goal-setting. Just like an athlete envisions crossing the finish line, you need to envision achieving your financial targets. Be specific. Saying you want to save money is like throwing a dart in the dark; saying you want to save $10,000 for a down payment on a house by next year gives you a clear target to aim for.

Don't underestimate the power of cutting back on the non-essentials. It's like trimming the fat – leaving you with a lean, mean, goal-funding machine. This might mean dining out less or even waiting for that movie to hit the streaming services instead of catching it in theaters. Prioritize experiences and purchases that feed your soul and move you closer to your big-picture life goals.

Inevitably, there will be roadblocks. Unexpected expenses loom just on the horizon, ready to throw a wrench into your neatly laid plans. This is why an emergency fund isn't just nice to have—it's a necessity. A financial buffer can keep you afloat when life's waves come crashing over you, letting you ride out the storm and get back on course.

Let's face it, life has a way of making budgeting feel like an anchor, dragging you down with its rigidity. But suppose you flip that perspective. View your budget as a map to hidden treasures. When you budget, you're marking the path to financial freedom, peace of mind, and those Eureka moments where dreams aren't just dreams anymore – they're the next stop on your personal odyssey.

Now, let's talk automation. Automating your savings is akin to hiring a personal assistant for your finances. Pre-arranged transfers to savings or investment accounts ensure you're always paying yourself first. Think of it as putting your success on autopilot.

In this interconnected world, not every expense comes annually or even monthly; some are sneakier, appearing quarterly or bi-annually. This is where the magic of the sinking fund comes into play. Allocate small amounts each month for these sporadic expenses, and when they roll around, you're ready. You'll surprise them – and yourself – with your readiness.

Saving is important, yes, but what about debt? Interest on debt can eat away at your resources like nothing else. Approach paying off debt like a chess game, strategizing your moves for maximum impact. Sometimes it means tackling the highest interest rates first; other times, it's about knocking out the smaller debts for the psychological wins that keep you motivated.

As you journey through life's twists and turns, remember to check in with your budget periodically. Life isn't static, and neither should your budget be. Adjust and pivot as needed. Perhaps you receive a raise, or your housing costs increase – your budget should reflect these changes in real-time.

Consider investing in budgeting tools or apps. They're the pocket-sized trainers for your financial health – keeping you in check and on task. Yes, mastering spreadsheets and financial software can be a bit of a learning curve, but the insights and clarity they offer can be game-changing. They're the modern armor in your quest for fiscal responsibility.

Lastly, make sure that within your budget, you create space for joy. A small indulgence, when budgeted for, isn't a setback; it's a much-needed release valve. It's a cool drink of water during your marathon. Manage your money such that it brings not only growth and stability but also a measure of happiness.

Let's not dance around it – budgeting can be tedious and demanding. But the individuals who make it to the top are the ones willing to do the work that others shy away from. They adjust their sails when the winds change, and keep their eyes on the horizon. They understand that to achieve something remarkable, they must plot their course with intention. That's what budgeting is all about – it's a steadfast commitment, a personal promise, to yourself and the brilliant future lying ahead.

Investing in Your Future

Investing in Your Future digs deep into the understanding that laying a financial foundation doesn't just happen overnight. It requires intention, insight, and often a bit of sacrifice. But here's the kicker – it's one of the most empowering things you'll ever do for yourself. Let's chat about how being smart with your money isn't about pinching pennies; it's about setting yourself free to make choices that allow you to live a life you love.

Investing isn't simply about the stock market or buying into the latest cryptocurrency trend. It's about understanding the value of your own potential. Your greatest asset in life isn't your bank account; it's you. Investing in your future starts with investing in yourself – your education, your health, and your relationships. Because when you're at your best, you're also at your most valuable.

Begin by taking stock of where you are now. What are your skills? How could they be sharper? Look into courses, books, or even a mentor who can help you get to that next level in your career. That's a solid investment. Every step you take to enhance your knowledge and abilities can open doors to opportunities you can't even imagine today.

Then, think for a moment about what actually makes you tick. Your passions are a clue to where you might want to direct your investments, both emotionally and financially. If you're driven by a cause, perhaps there's a way to back that passion with a financial investment. It could be a socially responsible fund, or even starting a small side business. When you invest in what you love, you're more likely to stay committed for the long haul.

Now, let's switch gears to more traditional forms of investing. Yes, making your money work for you is a big piece of this puzzle. If you've got debt, conquering it is your first move. After all, it's tough to grow your wealth if it's being nibbled away by high-interest payments. Then, when you're ready, ease into investing. You don't need a fortune to start; the beauty of compound interest means that even small amounts add up over time.

Diversification is your next magic word. Don't toss all your eggs in one basket. Spread out your investments across different asset classes, which can help protect you against major losses if one area turns sour. And hey, while we're at it, remember that not all investments are monetary. Time and energy devoted to building quality relationships can pay dividends in the form of support, advice, and opportunities.

Retirement may seem like a distant dream, but it won't stay that way forever. The sooner you begin to save for it, the more comfortable that dream life becomes. Take advantage of retirement accounts that offer tax perks, like a 401(k) or an IRA. It's not just about what you save, but also how those savings can grow through wise investments.

Emergency funds aren't the flashiest topic, but when life throws a curveball, you'll bless every cent you've tucked away. Aim to save enough to cover several months of living expenses. This safety net can keep you on stable ground, allowing you to take investment risks that can lead to bigger rewards.

Insurance is another cornerstone of your financial fortress. It's all about managing risk – whether that's your health, your property, or your life. Insurance helps ensure that a disaster doesn't derail your entire financial strategy.

Property can be a lucrative investment, but it requires doing your homework. Whether it's buying a home, investing in real estate, or even REITs (real estate investment trusts), property often appreciates over time. Plus, it can generate passive income if you choose to rent it out. Remember, location and timing are everything.

Never underestimate the power of passive income. This is how you earn money while you sleep – think rental income, dividends from stocks, or even royalties from creative work. Passive income streams can provide financial stability and freedom, allowing you to focus not just on making money, but making a life.

Speaking of making money, don't forget to negotiate your worth in the workplace. You are an investment to your employer, and ensuring you're properly compensated is key to your financial growth. Keep in mind that benefits like health insurance, retirement contributions, and performance bonuses are part of your compensation package. Don't leave money on the table.

Technology has revolutionized investing, making it more accessible than ever. You've got a whole arsenal of apps and tools that can help you track your spending, invest your cash, and monitor your progress. Knowledge is power, and with these resources at your fingertips, there's no excuse not to be informed about your financial health.

But remember, with great power comes great responsibility. The thrill of quick money can be enticing, but investing isn't about chasing the next big thing. It's about making thoughtful, informed decisions that align with your long-term vision. Get-rich-quick schemes are a dime a dozen, but true wealth is built steadily, with patience and determination.

Last but not least, an often overlooked aspect of investing is philanthropy. Generosity isn't just good for the soul; it can be savvy for your taxes too. More than that, investing in your community and causes you care about generates a kind of wealth that can't be measured in dollars – it's measured in impact and fulfillment.

You see, investing in your future is about so much more than stocks, bonds, and financial planning. It's about investing in a holistic vision of wealth that encompasses far more than just your bank account. It's about investing in a future that shines bright with possibility, stability, and joy.

Chapter 14

Mastering the Art of Negotiation

As we pivot from ensuring your financial prowess in the preceding chapter, we move into the intricate dance of negotiation—a skill pivotal to personal and professional growth. Mastering the art of negotiation isn't just about pushing for your terms, but rather about orchestrating a symphony of give-and-take that leaves everyone feeling valued. Think of it as the ultimate test of empathy, strategic thinking, and, above all, subtle persuasion. Hone in on listening, not just to reply but to understand the often unspoken needs and interests that fuel the other side's stance. Remember, every interaction is an opportunity to forge alliances that can propel you to your goals. A delicate balance of assertiveness and flexibility is key; there's an art to holding your ground while allowing the other party to feel like a winner, too. Imagine each successful negotiation not just as a win for today but as a stepping stone to the lifelong partnerships that will carry you toward your larger vision. Master this, and you've unlocked a treasure trove of opportunities waiting to be tapped into at every turn.

Strategies for Successful Deals

Strategies for Successful Deals hinge on the foundation you've been cultivating throughout this evocative journey. Successful deals aren't solely about numbers and contracts; they're about relationships, foresight, and an intrinsic understanding of your goals and limits. As you step into the art of negotiation, there are core strategies that can propel you toward successful outcomes.

First and foremost, *preparation* is key. Enter any negotiation with a thorough understanding of the other party's needs, wants, and pain points. Your prep work should include researching the market, understanding industry standards, and having a clear picture of the outcome you want. Knowledge isn't just power; it's tactical advantage.

Building rapport cannot be overstated. People want to deal with those they know, like, and trust. So, before you dive into the hard talk, spend time establishing a connection. Relating on a human level can make or break the dynamics of a negotiation.

Set clear goals before you enter the negotiation room. However, also understand the concept of BATNA—Best Alternative to a Negotiated Agreement. Knowing your walk-away point and alternatives ensures that you don't agree to a deal you'll later regret. It's not just about winning; it's about securing a win that aligns with your greater vision.

Then, anchor your negotiations. Start by putting forward a strong but fair proposal. This sets the stage for the negotiation and can often bring the other party closer to your ideal outcome. Hone in on what's in their best interest, showing how your proposal aligns with their goals as well.

Listening is a tool just as crucial as speaking. Active listening involves paying full attention, asking clarifying questions, and reflecting back what you've heard. It not only shows respect but also helps pinpoint what's truly driving the other party's stance.

Effective negotiators master the dance of empathy. Understanding the other side's viewpoint without necessarily agreeing with it can unlock paths to mutual satisfaction. Empathy builds bridges and can guide you to creative resolutions.

Throughout a negotiation, look for the win-win. Find solutions that benefit both parties. This isn't just feel-good rhetoric; it's strategic long-term thinking. Today's counterpart could be tomorrow's partner—or referral source. Sustainable deals are rooted in mutual benefit.

Don't shy away from making concessions, but make them strategically. When you give something up, ensure the other party understands the value of what they're gaining. And, when possible, get something in return each time you concede.

It's also essential to remain calm and composed. No matter how tense negotiations get, losing your temper can significantly weaken your position. Practicing patience and maintaining a steady demeanor showcase strength and confidence.

Know that bluffing is a double-edged sword. Trust is the currency of negotiation, so use falsehoods sparingly and carefully. Authenticity typically has a higher long-term payout than a short-lived tactical gain achieved through deceit.

Don't be afraid to pause and regroup when discussions come to a standstill. Take a time-out to reassess your position and strategy. Reflection away from the bargaining table can provide new insights and alternatives.

In some cases, using silence as a tool can be incredibly powerful. Not every pause needs to be filled. Silence can prompt contemplation, encourage the other party to speak more, or even concede certain points.

Remember to focus on interests, not positions. Identifying the underlying interests on both sides reveals the common ground and opens the door to agreement. Deals are done not just on figures but on fulfilling needs.

Documentation is vital. Once you've arrived at an agreement, get it in writing as soon as possible. A verbal agreement is valuable, but written confirmation is essential to ensure all parties stick to their promises and understand their obligations.

Lastly, whether you walk away with a deal or not, take time to reflect on the experience. Learning from each negotiation, successful or not, is what propels growth. Consolidate your gains, analyze missteps, and always, always keep honing your skills for the next round. Your journey towards becoming a master of negotiation is ongoing; embrace each step with the zeal of a winner who's always hungry for improvement.

Win-Win Scenarios

Imagine stepping into a negotiation with confidence, armed with strategies that not only promise success for yourself but also bring value to everyone involved. That's the heart and soul of creating a win-win scenario: harnessing the power of negotiation so that everyone leaves the table satisfied. The art of negotiation isn't just about taking; it's about exchanging value in a manner that all parties can shake hands with a sense of true accomplishment.

Now, this might sound idealistic. And you're right; the world of negotiation is often portrayed as cutthroat, a place where only the ruthless make it to the top. But that narrative is shifting. The new champions in any field understand that success isn't about bulldozing through to get what you want at the cost of relationships and reputation. Instead, it's about finding that sweet spot where mutual needs are met, and mutual goals are reached.

To get there, begin by genuinely understanding the other party's needs and wants. It's about active listening, which we already talked about in a previous chapter. When you truly listen, you're not just waiting for your turn to speak. You're hearing the words, reading between the lines, and grasping what's left unsaid. That understanding becomes your blueprint for crafting an agreement that appeals to the shared interests rather than the dividing lines.

Think about the last time you faced resistance. Perhaps it was in a team meeting, a family decision, or even a sales pitch. Did you push harder, or did you step back to reconceptualize the offer from the other person's perspective? The trick is to pivot your approach so that you present your ideas as solutions to their concerns or as opportunities to achieve their desires.

Empathy is your ally here. It's the ability to place yourself in someone else's shoes and view the world from their vantage point. When you negotiate with empathy, you're not manipulating; you're collaborating. You're finding the intersecting points of your ambitions and forging a path that benefits both sides. You're not just building agreements; you're building relationships.

And let's talk about flexibility. A rigid mindset will see you knocked down by the winds of change, but flexibility allows you to sway and adapt. Negotiations can be unpredictable, and your willingness to alter your approach or offer can transform a deadlocked situation into a successful compromise. Like bamboo, strong yet bendable, this attribute can define your growth in any negotiation.

Another essential aspect is creativity. You could stick to the script, or you could innovate your way into new possibilities that haven't been considered yet. This isn't about pulling a rabbit out of a hat; it's about merging perspectives to invent solutions that cater to both parties. Sometimes the best agreements are those that create a new reality that didn't exist before the negotiation began.

So, let's not forget the importance of transparency. Games and deceptions can lead to short-term gains, but they're a poor strategy for lasting success. Clear, open communication about your goals, abilities, and limitations paves the way for trust. And trust is the currency of lasting win-win scenarios. It's simple: people do business with those they like and trust.

Now, in your journey to crafting win-win scenarios, remember to have patience. An eagerness to close the deal quickly can result in overlooking details or making concessions that aren't in your best interest. Patience allows for thoughtful consideration, thorough discussion, and the discovery of the most compatible avenues for agreement.

The negotiation table is also a learning environment. Every interaction teaches you something about people, business, and even yourself. It's about incremental growth and knowledge that you can carry over to your next negotiation, and the one after that. See each negotiation as a stepping stone to mastering the art of the win-win scenario.

Now, one might wonder, is every negotiation scenario capable of being win-win? The truth is, not all of them will be. But your aim is to push the boundaries towards positive-sum outcomes as much as possible. It's a mindset, a commitment to integrity, and a demonstration of respect for those you engage with. This approach sets the foundation for positive, ongoing relationships that could open doors for future negotiations and collaborations.

Let's not forget the role of confidence. It's about believing in the value you bring to the table. When you're confident, it's contagious. Others will believe in your proposals because you do. Confidence isn't about arrogance; it's about assurance of the benefits of the solutions you're proposing for all involved.

And finally, know when to walk away. There's strength in recognizing that not all negotiations will, or should, end in agreement. Some proposals don't align with your values or long-term goals, and it's alright to respectfully step back. This courage not to force a fit protects you from arrangements that could become losses in disguise.

Crafting win-win scenarios isn't just a skill. It's an approach to life, a testament to the belief that when one wins, it doesn't have to come at the loss of another. As we carry this philosophy into all aspects of our lives, we become not just champions in our field but champions of a better, more collaborative world where victory is shared and savored together.

Chapter 15

Leading like a Champion

Transitioning from the individual play of mastering negotiations, we step onto the field of leadership, that relentless pursuit where the heartbeat of success pulses not just within ourselves, but resonates through others. If greatness is our collective goal, then let's talk about leading—yet not just any kind of leading but one that leaves a mark, an impression, an inspiration that outlasts the initial moment of triumph. Leading like a champion means you're lighting fires in the bellies of those around you, fostering a spirit that enables them to tap into their latent potential, driving them indefinitely towards their own pinnacles of success. It's less about commanding and more about connecting, less about dictating, and more about demonstrating. A true champion's leadership style is like gravity—it pulls rather than pushes; it anchors and gives everything else its rightful place. It isn't always about the trophies or the accolades; sometimes, it's about nurturing growth, celebrating the collective efforts, and perhaps most importantly, leaving a legacy of such potent leadership that the light you've ignited continues to blaze, forging new paths long after you've passed the torch.

Inspirational Leadership

Inspirational Leadership is not just about taking the helm and steering the ship; it's an art form that calls to the deepest desires and highest aspirations of all those you lead. It's about lighting that spark within others so they can find their path to victory, alongside yours, creating a symphony of success that resonates through every challenge.

Consider the greatest leaders you know; they have a magnetic quality that goes beyond charisma. It's as if they breathe life into dreams and turn doubts into stepping stones. How do they do it? Authenticity is key. They show up as their true selves, vulnerabilities and all, inspiring trust, and fostering an environment where everyone feels they belong and their contribution is valued.

They are also visionaries, crafting a compelling future that excites and mobilizes. A vision is not just a destination; it's a beckoning force that draws you forth when the journey gets tough. Inspirational leaders articulate this vision with such clarity and passion that it becomes a shared mission, not just a personal goal.

Of course, shaping a vision is only the start—inspirational leaders galvanize action. They're adept at translating the grand picture into small, actionable steps, making the impossible seem achievable. They empower by delegating, trusting their team members with critical tasks, and guiding them to take risks and expand their capabilities.

Such leaders are also consummate storytellers. They weave narratives that celebrate past triumphs and frame future adventures, illustrating the role each person plays in this collective journey. Storytelling is a potent tool that helps maintain motivation and reminds people of the 'why' behind their hard work.

A leader's communication skills are instrumental in inspiration. It's not just about speaking with confidence; it's about actively listening, empathizing, and responding in ways that encourage open dialogue. This two-way communication ensures that team members feel heard and understood, further cementing their commitment to shared goals.

In the face of adversity, inspirational leaders shine brightest, exuding a resilience that becomes contagious. They confront challenges head-on, all while maintaining positivity, nurturing hope, and leading by example. Their attitude shows that every hurdle is an opportunity for growth and learning.

Moreover, they recognize that success is not a solo endeavor. By highlighting the achievements of individuals and the group, they foster a culture of appreciation and celebration. Acknowledgements and kudos, whether in private or public, serve as the fuel that keeps the team's spirits high and aspirations soaring.

Inspiring leadership also involves a commitment to continual growth and development. Leaders often pour into their own personal and professional growth, creating a ripple effect that encourages their team to also pursue lifelong learning. It's about modeling the behavior you wish to see, becoming a lighthouse of possibility.

Their approach to problem-solving is another facet that sets them apart. Inspirational leaders think creatively, welcome innovation, and are never too proud to seek insights from various sources, thereby fostering a team culture where out-of-the-box thinking is not just accepted, but expected and encouraged.

Importantly, an inspirational leader understands the power of empathy. They connect on a human level, sharing in the joys and sorrows of their team. This emotional connection breeds loyalty and a sense of unity, reinforcing that none are alone in their struggles or their successes.

A true mark of such a leader is the ability to admit mistakes. By owning up to their errors and taking responsibility, they set a standard of accountability and integrity that elevates the whole team. It's the antithesis of blame culture, and it paves the way for honest and progressive conversations.

In the realm of inspiration, the leader's well-being is just as important as their team's. They set boundaries, prioritize their health, and maintain balance, showing it's possible to chase success without burning out. Self-care is not selfish; it's the foundation that allows them to lead effectively and sustainably.

Finally, inspirational leaders are future-focused but present-centered. They help the team prepare for what's to come, while also emphasizing the importance of the current moment—the only time where action can truly be taken. Bringing mindfulness into the workplace, they forge a culture of presence and focus that drives productivity.

While this journey of inspirational leadership demands much, the rewards are immeasurable—not just in terms of accomplishments but in the richness of relationships and the personal growth of everyone involved. As you lead, you don't just reach for your own potential—you unlock the greatness in others, and together, you create a legacy of champions.

Empowering Others to Succeed

Empowering Others to Succeed speaks to the heart of leadership, which is not just about personal triumphs but also about lifting others as we ascend. Imagine holding a lantern; it loses no light by lighting another. This concept is similar in empowering others; by helping someone else shine, your light doesn't dim—it grows brighter, illuminating paths for many. Pathfinders have often cited the fulfillment that comes from watching someone they've nurtured reach their goals. It's not just a feel-good factor; it holds a profound truth about success and leadership.

There's a common misconception that to be successful, you need to put yourself first—always. But the ever-evolving landscape of success tells us something different. It whispers of a world where your own victory is interwoven with the success of others. There's something magical about the shared triumphs and the interdependency that fuels high-performing teams and communities. So, let's talk about what it truly means to empower others and how it's a winning strategy for everyone involved.

First off, recognize the potential in those around you. It's easy to overlook, especially when competition stiffens and personal goals demand all your focus. But there's immense power in noticing someone's unpolished talent or untapped potential and taking a moment to nurture it. You don't have to be a seasoned coach or mentor to encourage someone. Sometimes, a simple acknowledgment or a piece of advice at the right time can act as the catalyst for someone else's breakthrough.

Communication plays a pivotal role in empowerment. Active listening, which we've dissected earlier, isn't just about comprehending others. It's also about making people feel heard and valued. When you engage in meaningful exchanges, you create an environment where people are more likely to take initiative and strive. People flourish when they feel their input is respected and their contributions make a difference.

Another vital element to consider is delegation. It might be tempting to keep the reins firmly in your hands, especially if you have perfectionist leanings. But delegation is about more than just lightening your workload. It's an act of trust, offering others a platform to rise to the occasion. Think of it as investing in their growth, and as they succeed, they expand your collective capacity for achievement.

Feedback is a two-way street, and when it comes to empowering others, it's all about the delivery. Constructive criticism is a builder, while destructive is a bulldozer. Choose to build. Foster an environment where feedback is seen as a growth opportunity, and watch as it motivates rather than discourages.

Then there's the art of recognition. Celebrating small wins and acknowledging effort encourages a culture of perseverance and dedication. When people feel like their efforts are seen and appreciated, they are more likely to push beyond their boundaries and set new bars for excellence.

Growth happens at the edges of our comfort zones, and sometimes people need a little nudge to venture there. Challenging someone with a task they haven't tried before or setting a higher bar than they set for themselves can spark their journey of self-discovery. However, balance is key. It's important to ensure that the challenges are within reach and that you're there to provide support as they stretch towards them.

Collaboration, rather than competition, fosters a breeding ground for innovation and collective problem solving. When you empower others, your leadership is no longer defined by your ability to outshine but by your capability to unify and harness the diverse strengths of a group. Remember, winners are not threatened by someone else's ability but are invigorated by the synergy that it brings.

Let's talk about trust. It's the foundation upon which empowerment is built. When you show faith in someone's ability to make decisions or think creatively, you're not just passing off responsibility; you're validating their competence and encouraging their independence. It's a message that says, 'You've got this, and I believe in you.' That level of faith from a leader can be transformative.

But with trust comes the need for patience. People will make mistakes—it's an irreplaceable part of the learning process. As a leader, your reaction to these mistakes can either cultivate resilience and learning or instill fear of trying. By choosing to view mistakes as valuable learning moments, you set the stage for growth and continuous improvement.

Educating and facilitating continuous learning for your team or the individuals around you is another way to empower others. Sharing knowledge and providing resources for others to expand their skills doesn't just enhance their capabilities; it also shows that you have a vested interest in their personal and professional growth.

When you empower others, you're not just fostering their success — you're setting up a domino effect. The confidence and skills that you instill in them will, in turn, inspire them to empower others. This creates an ever-expanding cycle of growth and success, building a legacy that outlasts individual achievements.

Lastly, empowerment is a reflection of humility. It takes a secure leader to elevate others with the confidence that their rise will not overshadow but rather cast a wider light. It's a mark of a victorious leader, not just on paper or in their own narrative but in the enduring success stories they've helped to write in the pages of others' careers and lives.

To conclude, empowering others is where true leadership spirit and success combine. It's seeing beyond the horizon of self-interest into a landscape where collective victories contribute to personal achievements. Empowering others to succeed is more than a practice; it's a philosophy—a true champion's creed. By uplifting those around us, we don't just climb ladders; we build towers that stand the test of time, stories high, with foundations strengthened by shared success and mutual support.

Chapter 16

Innovation

Thinking Outside the Box

With the grit of resilience and the grace of a winner's positivity, let's pivot to a realm where the ordinary doesn't cut it—innovation. It's about giving that mental box a good shake, tipping it over, and peering into the corners we've ignored. Innovation isn't just a flashy buzzword; it's the pulse that keeps our dreams vibrant in a world that's constantly changing. We're not just talking about inventors and tech gurus; it's about each one of us tapping into our creative veins, finding novel solutions to age-old problems, and adapting like chameleons to whatever curveball life pitches. Through innovation, we find a way to surf on the waves of change instead of being swept away. So let's peel away the layers of convention and explore how offbeat thinking can paint our goals in colors more brilliant than we could have imagined.

Creative Problem-Solving

Creative Problem-Solving is an art that champions in every field master, not by magic, but through continuous development and innovative thinking. And here's the thing, you have the same capability within you. It starts with seeing challenges not just as obstacles, but as opportunities to flex your creative muscles and devise solutions that soar above conventional thinking. This chapter will guide you to harness your innate problem-solving abilities in new and exciting ways.

Now, visualize a maze. Those twists, turns, dead ends? They represent the problems we face in life. Most see a single path through the maze, but the creatives see the walls as mere suggestions. They're not bound to simply follow; they leap over, tunnel under, or even break down the walls. This is the essence of creative problem-solving; not just selecting from ready-made solutions but crafting your own unique responses to challenges.

Let's begin by shattering a common myth: creative problem-solving isn't restricted to those in 'creative' professions. Whether you're an entrepreneur, a corporate executive, or a stay-at-home parent, every scenario you face can be approached with a creative mindset. It's not about your job title; it's about your approach to the hurdles life places in your path.

First things first, though, creativity thrives on a rich bed of diverse experiences. It's intertwined with curiosity – a willingness to ask questions, explore, and dismantle the status quo. Have you been feeding your curiosity lately? Think of it as planting seeds that, when nurtured, will sprout ideas you didn't even know you were capable of conceiving.

Okay, say you're staring down an issue that feels insurmountable. Standard solutions haven't worked, and you're at a standstill. Here's where the magic starts. Instead of asking "Why isn't this working?", flip it: "In what ways can this work differently?" It's a subtle shift in questioning, but it opens up a world of possibilities, sparking thoughts and ideas that may have been lurking in the back of your mind, waiting for their moment to shine.

The road to effective creative problem-solving is paved with brainstorming – not the old-fashioned 'everyone throw in an idea' sort, but structured, directed brainstorming. It's about generating quantity over quality at first. Set yourself a timer and just let the ideas flow without restraint. It's in this unfettered state that our minds can make connections we might otherwise overlook.

Still, creativity isn't a solo act. Collaborate. Innovation often sparks brighter in a group where one thought leads to another, forming a chain reaction of creativity. Diverse perspectives can illuminate unseen angles to a problem, providing breakthroughs you couldn't have reached on your own. Remember, it's about building on each other's thoughts, not competing for the so-called 'best' idea.

But what happens when you hit a creative block? Even the most adept problem-solvers sometimes find their minds hitting a wall. Here's a tip: take a break. It might seem counterintuitive, but stepping away from a problem can sometimes bring you closer to a solution. Engage in something unrelated; dance, paint, go for a walk, anything that shifts your focus. Often, it's during these moments that the solution quietly drops into your lap.

Tools, of course, are a creative problem-solver's best friend. Mind maps, flowcharts, or even simple lists can visualize the problem and potential solutions. These tools help organize your thoughts, making connections more apparent and helping you to think laterally.

Don't forget the power of reframing. Sometimes problems persist not because they're unsolvable, but because they're not understood deeply enough. Look at the issue from different angles, through different lenses.

Question your assumptions. You might find that the problem wasn't what you thought it was at all.

Now, backing up these creative efforts should be a solid bedrock of knowledge. Stay informed. Understand the context of your problem, and research similar challenges faced by others. Knowledge fuels creativity, giving you a springboard from which you can leap into the realm of innovative solutions.

And when you have a potential solution, prototype it. Create a small-scale model or enact a micro-version of your idea. It's alright if it fails – remember earlier chapters discussed the importance of learning from failure? This is where that mindset pays off. Each failed prototype is simply a step closer to a workable solution.

A crucial aspect often overlooked is setting the environment conducive to creativity. Is your workspace, both physical and mental, cluttered? A clean space allows for clear thinking. A positive, open environment encourages risk-taking in thought - an essential ingredient in creative problem-solving.

Resilience, as discussed earlier, also plays a key role here. Creative solutions often require boldness to implement. If you float an unconventional idea and it falls flat at first, don't retreat. Be ready to stand by your creativity, to tweak, adjust, and try again with the same enthusiasm.

Lastly, embracing and fostering a culture of creativity around you can ensure a steady flow of ideas. Encourage those you work with to think creatively, challenge norms, and not fear proposing solutions that seem outlandish at first. As you build this culture, you'll find that your own creative problem-solving skills will sharpen as you're no longer an island of creativity but part of a continent buzzing with innovative energy.

An entire spectrum of potential lies within you, untapped and often unacknowledged. Creative problem-solving isn't just a skill - it's a perspective, a way of life that you can embrace fully. Allow yourself to see not just with your eyes, but with your imagination. It's there, in the boundless playground of your mind, that you'll find the answers you seek, the paths less traveled, and the solutions that will not just lead you to success but define what success means to you. The transformational journey of becoming a problem-solver of extraordinary capability starts with a simple step: believe in your ability to create, and then set forth to do just that.

Adapting to Change

Adapting to change is sort of like learning to surf. You've got your surfboard, which is all the skills and knowledge you've accumulated in life, and you're out there on the ocean, facing the waves. As you already know, no two waves are the same. Just like the changes and challenges life throws our way. To stay upright, to master the ride, you've got to be flexible, adapt your stance, and sometimes, when the big ones come, pivot completely.

One of the inescapable truths about life is its constant state of flux. The skill to embrace and adapt to changes is a hallmark of champion minds; they understand the dance with change is unending. Change spans from the predictable to the utterly unexpected, the minute to the monumental. And it's not just about accepting change; it's about mastering the art of transformation, so you move with it, using it to propel you forward instead of becoming a roadblock.

We're living in times where the ability to adapt is crucial. The landscape of work, life, and relationships is evolving more rapidly than ever before. Let's not kid ourselves; adaptation can be tough, especially when change comes uninvited. But those who thrive, not just survive, cultivate adaptability as a core strength. Adaptation is a muscle, and like any muscle, it strengthens with use.

To start adapting better, let's first dispense with the idea that we have total control over our environments and ourselves. Life's full of surprises, and some of the most profound growth experiences come from circumstances we didn't design. Instead of clinging to control, why not focus on what we can influence—our responses to change?

Notice how top performers in any field adjust their strategies based on new information or unexpected outcomes. They're less likely to fall apart when they encounter a snag because they've fostered this adaptability. Instead of hammering away with what used to work, they pause, assess, and adapt. This same principle applies to all areas of life—be it personal relationships, career development, or self-care.

When change is imminent, do you dig your heels in and resist, or do you lean into the discomfort and look for the opportunities it presents? History is littered with examples of individuals and companies that failed because they refused to adapt. Let's not be part of that narrative. Let's be part of the story where change is an ally, a catalyst for innovation and personal evolution.

Consider change in the workplace. As markets shift and technologies advance, so must our skill sets. Those who climb the career ladder fastest aren't necessarily those with the deepest expertise in one area, but those who can pivot, learn quickly, and apply themselves anew. This isn't just about professional resiliency, it's about vibrant, dynamic career progression.

How about those personal transformations? Maybe you've gone through or are in the midst of one now—a change in family dynamics, a health journey, or a re-evaluation of what truly matters to you. These changes can feel seismic, disorienting even. But they're also incredible opportunities to reassess, to realign with your values, and to carve out a life more deeply attuned to who you are and who you want to be.

One strategy for adapting to change is to foster a mindset of learning. Adopt the perspective that every change is a learning opportunity, a chance to acquire new understanding, new strategies, and new insights. The winners in life aren't the ones who never fail or face change; they're the ones who learn with every curveball thrown their way.

Another potent tool for adaptability is developing a versatile skill set. In times of change, transferable skills become your safest bet. They're the currency that remains valuable no matter where life takes you. This might mean honing soft skills like communication, leadership, or problem-solving, which apply broadly across various aspects of life.

Transitions will happen; that's a given. So, start building your support systems now. Friends, family, mentors—they can all provide valuable perspective and guidance. Sharing the load can turn an overwhelming wave of change into a challenge that's approached with a team spirit.

Let's also talk about stress, because let's face it, change can be stressful. But stress can be a useful signal; it can be the body's way of saying, "Hey, pay attention!" So instead of trying to eliminate stress, let's use it to heighten our awareness and prepare us to address whatever's coming our way. Mindfulness, meditation, and stress reduction strategies are powerful allies in calibrating our response to change.

Finally, while adapting to change, we must have grace for ourselves. Not every adaptation will be smooth or successful on the first try. There will be floundering, there'll be wipeouts. And that's ok—in fact, it's expected. It's through these less-than-perfect attempts that we truly learn and build the resilience needed for long-term success.

In this rapidly changing world, remember that your ability to adapt is not just a strategy for coping—it's a strategy for thriving. The more we can embrace change, the more we open ourselves up to the vast potential of the life we're living. Here's to mastering the waves, to adjusting our sails when the winds change, and to approaching life's endless transformations with determination, flexibility, and grace.

As we conclude this discussion on adaptation, let's not forget that the next chapter awaits, promising to build on these adaptive techniques. Embracing change isn't an isolated endeavor; it's integrated deeply within the larger picture of innovation, technological proficiency, continuous learning, and the quest for a fulfilled life. And isn't that the essence of winning—at home, work, and within ourselves?

Chapter 17

The Digital Champion
Leveraging Technology

As we've fine-tuned our mindset and refined our approach to success in prior chapters, it can't be overstated how modern technology sits at the forefront of this journey—especially with the surge in digital connectivity. It's high time we embrace it not as a distraction, but as a powerful ally. Imagine being able to reach a network as vast as the ocean with a tap of your finger, or crafting an online persona that resonates with your core values and beams them across the globe. Yes, technology can be overwhelming, its waves hitting us from every direction, but within that ceaseless tide lies endless possibilities. By becoming a digital champion, we're not just riding the crest of innovation; we're shaping our destinies with the tools of our time. This isn't about being tech-savvy for the sake of it; it's about strategically utilizing platforms to build a personal brand, amplify your voice, and create opportunities that align with your winning vision. When wielded wisely, the digital world accelerates our paths to excellence, setting up networks, resources, and communities that can catapult you towards the podium of your potential.

Social Media for Success

In the digital age, leveraging social media isn't just about staying connected; it's a powerful tool to catapult you towards your goals. Consider this: platforms buzzing with millions of users can transform from spaces of casual scrolling to arenas where victories are born. The key lies in deliberate, strategic engagement that underscores your journey towards excellence.

Think about social media as a stage upon which your personal brand plays out. Every tweet, every post, and every story you share pieces together a mosaic of who you are and what you stand for. Craft your online presence with the same care you would approach any aspect of your championship life.

To begin with, clarity is paramount. Recognize your mission and the audience you wish to reach. Whether it's LinkedIn for professional connections or Instagram to showcase your creative side, each platform offers distinct advantages. Tailor your content to align with your goals and the interests of your followers, always aiming to provide value that resonates.

Interaction on social media should be more than just a broadcast of your achievements. Engage in meaningful conversations, contribute thoughtfully to discussions, and listen actively to your community. The connections you forge through authentic interaction could be the next bridge to an opportunity previously unseen.

Building a robust community on social media also means being consistent. Your online presence is a reflection of your dedication. Regularly sharing insights, triumphs, and even setbacks — with an attitude of learning and growth, of course — builds trust and keeps you top of mind with your network.

A CHAMPION'S MINDSET

And let's not overlook the power of collaboration. Social media can be fertile ground for partnerships. By cross-promoting with others who share your values and vision, the potential for growth and reach is magnified. Like any championship team, mutual support is a cornerstone of sustained success.

Now, with all this engagement, it's equally essential to be mindful of your digital well-being. Allocate specific times for social media to prevent it from encroaching on other critical areas of champion living, like deep work or quality time with loved ones. Manage your time online; don't let it manage you.

Furthermore, it demands raising your voice for good. Being a champion isn't only about personal growth; it's leading by example. Foster an environment that encourages positive change, be it by advocating for a cause close to your heart or by lifting others' spirits with hopeful messaging. This is how thought leaders are shaped — not with loudness, but with significance.

When we speak of weaving stories, the narrative is everything. Your journey, filled with its nuances of victory and struggle, is unique. Share it! Humanize your triumphs and admit to your defeats. The authenticity it brings to social media can not only inspire others but also define you as resilient and relatable — a real champion.

Critical to all of this is your digital literacy. Keeping up to date with the latest trends and best practices in social media ensures you stay relevant, effective, and secure. A winner's mindset involves a commitment to continuous learning — the digital landscape is no exception.

Visual content can speak volumes. A compelling image, a well-produced video, or an insightful infographic can grab attention far more effectively than text alone. In the fast-paced stream of social feeds, vibrant visuals can be the difference between scrolling past or stopping to engage.

Despite the glitz and the viral hopes, remember not every post has to set the internet on fire. Patience and perspective are virtues. Consistency and perseverance bear fruit over time, and while viral content may spike your metrics, the steady cultivation of your brand lays the groundwork for sustained impact.

With all these elements in play, evaluation becomes critical. Use analytics to your advantage. Measure your social media performance, understand what works, and learn from what doesn't. Data-driven decisions can pivot your strategy from good to game-changing.

And yes, with visibility comes vulnerability. Be prepared for criticism and navigate it with grace and poise. Distinguish between constructive feedback that propels you forward and noise that needs to be tuned out. This discernment keeps your focus sharp and your journey forward steady.

Therefore, encompassing social media into your blueprint for success is not about chasing likes or followers. It's a strategic, measured, and authentic extension of your championship-caliber life. When managed with intention and wisdom, it's a conduit to opportunities, a chronicle of growth, a showcase of leadership, and a testament to the unwavering spirit of a true champion.

Personal Branding Online

In an age where digital footprints are as critical as the shoes we wear, establishing a personal brand online isn't just smart; it's essential. Think of it as crafting your own legend, your unique trademark in the vast interconnected world.

Personal branding online starts with understanding oneself. It's delving into the core of your passions, skills, and values. It requires a clear vision of how you want to be perceived and what you want to achieve. This echoes back to the power of goal setting discussed earlier; knowing your destination is the first step to getting there.

An effective online brand is authentic. Transparency resonates deeply with the digital audience. They can sniff out pretense from a mile away. So, ensure that your online persona is a true reflection of who you are. Embrace your quirks and share your journey; it's these human elements that foster genuine connections.

Your personal brand should also echo the fundamentals of resilience, a concept we've touched on in previous chapters. It's the image of bouncing back from adversities and redefining failures that makes your brand relatable and inspiring. Channeling positivity online is a beacon that attracts followers and creates a support network around you.

Consistency is key in personal branding. Your online presence should reflect a coherent story across platforms, whether it's LinkedIn, Twitter, or Instagram. The routine of posting regularly and engaging with your audience fosters recognition and trust. And just as a disciplined approach is crucial in achieving excellence, it applies to maintaining an influential online presence.

Finding your 'why' also translates to a compelling brand narrative. Why do you do what you do? Why should someone follow you or believe in your brand? Answering these questions online with clarity and passion is magnetic. It's what separates the memorable from the forgettable in the digital space.

Understanding and conquering fear are components of our journey thus far. Similarly, pushing past the fear of judgment online is crucial. Venturing into the vulnerable territory of putting your personal brand out there can be daunting, but it's a bravery that pays dividends. It's about silencing that inner critic and speaking out with confidence.

Optimism isn't just a winner's secret weapon in life; it's influential in crafting your online narrative. Highlight the bright spots, champion your strengths, and express gratitude for the support and opportunities. People gravitate toward the light, and a positive online persona can be that shining beacon.

As for building winning relationships, your personal brand should strive to reflect a networker with purpose. Online connections made with intention can lead to mentorships, collaborations, and growth opportunities. Just as in the physical world, the bonds you cultivate digitally can become your strongest advocates.

Effective communication is as crucial online as it is in person. The way you articulate your thoughts, respond to comments, and convey your messages through the written word defines your brand. It's not just what you say; it's how you say it that counts.

Another vital component is leveraging your personal brand for health and well-being advocacy. Sharing your journey toward peak performance, stress management, and the balance beam of life can inspire others. It demonstrates a holistic approach to success, encompassing the champion's mindset with a lifestyle that supports it.

The digital realm allows for innovation in how you present your brand. Thinking outside the box and finding creative ways to engage your audience sets you apart. Whether it's through video content, infographics, or interactive posts, diverse methods of communication can enhance your brand's appeal.

Lifelong education resonates online as well. Sharing insights, lessons learned, and continuing your quest for knowledge demonstrates thought leadership and a commitment to growth. Your digital presence should serve as a testimony to your open-mindedness and your continuous pursuit of improvement.

Mindfulness and presence are just as impactful in the online sphere. In a world saturated with fleeting attention, showing a mindful approach to interactions and content creation can be your hallmark. It signals a depth that transcends the ephemeral nature of digital noise.

Your personal brand online is not only about showcasing your accomplishments but also about recognizing and celebrating the wins of others. Sharing and congratulating peers on their successes fosters community and demonstrates leadership that doesn't shy away from lifting others. It encapsulates the spirit of sustainable success, where winning is about growing together.

Embarking on personal branding online is more than constructing an image; it's about sculpting your digital legacy. Your online persona becomes the narrative of your journey, reflecting the resilience, positivity, and authenticity you carry within. Remember, the virtual world is your arena, and your brand is your unique signature move. It's time to shine, sharing that unmistakable essence of who you are for the world to see and applaud.

Chapter 18

Continuous Learning
Stay Ahead of the Game

Just as the last chords of one song set the stage for the next, transitioning seamlessly from mastering the digital world in Chapter 17, we now pivot to the realm of *continuous learning*, a cornerstone to remaining competitive in this ever-dynamic life. Imagine your potential if your thirst for knowledge never quenched; if every day, you integrated pieces of wisdom from all around. This isn't just about formal education or climbing the corporate ladder—it's an invitation to enrich the tapestry of your life with threads of insight from a myriad of sources. From teenage tech prodigies to the seasoned tales of our elders, information is ripe for the taking. By choosing to be students of life, we keep our skills sharp, our minds nimble, and our innovative spirits ablaze. Although it's tempting to rest on our laurels, remember—there's room to grow, and the horizon of knowledge is boundless. Don't just play the game; stay ahead of it by etching continuous learning into the very fabric of your journey.

Lifelong Education: Fuel for the Flame of Success

Think back to the feeling of crossing the finish line, not just at the end of a race, but at every milestone achieved. It's invigorating, isn't it? That sensation is the essence of what lifelong education can bring to every aspect of our lives—constantly crossing new finish lines and setting the bar higher each time. Lifelong education isn't about sitting in a classroom forever; it's about maintaining a mindset that is open to absorbing new knowledge, learning new skills, and expanding one's perspective indefinitely. It's making the conscious choice to be a perpetual learner, a relentless seeker of growth and improvement.

Imagine for a moment that your mind is a garden. Just as you would with any garden, you want it to flourish. This requires regular nurturing, weeding out the unnecessary, and planting new seeds of knowledge and experience. Lifelong education is that ongoing cultivation. But why is it so crucial? The world we live in is ever-changing, every moment bustling with innovation and thought. Staying educated is how you remain relevant, not just in your career but in life itself.

So, you've mastered your daily routine, built resilient habits, and you've tapped into the wellspring of motivation. Excellent! Now, let's talk about how lifelong education intertwines with these foundational pieces. It's one thing to set a goal, visualize success, and establish a winning mindset. But how do you continue to scale new heights once you've reached what you thought was the peak?

The answer lies in constantly seeking new knowledge. And it's not just academic learning we're talking about. It's a broader, more encompassing education. It's reading extensively, diving into books that challenge your ideas and expose you to new thinking. It's attending workshops, conferences, and talks to connect with pioneers and like-minded growth-seekers. It's experimenting with online courses and embracing the vast digital world to acquire skills at your fingertips.

It's important to remember that learning isn't merely an intake of information. It's also about pondering, questioning, and debating. It's as much about engaging with what you learn as it is about the learning itself. Scrutinize new information, verify its validity, and make it relevant to you. Apply what you've learned to real-world situations, whether that's testing a new communication technique you've read about or a management skill you've picked up from a podcast.

Another critical aspect of lifelong education is to nurture creativity and innovation. How? By stepping outside your comfort zone. Take a class in something totally unrelated to your field. Learn a new language. Pick up an instrument. The neural gymnastics of acquiring new, seemingly unrelated skills can foster creative connections that benefit all areas of life, personally and professionally.

An often overlooked part of lifelong education is reflection. After immersing yourself in new experiences or information, take a step back. Reflect on what these learnings mean for you. How can they be integrated into your practice? How do they alter your perspective? Reflection solidifies learning and empowers you to make informed choices moving forward.

Did you know that teaching others is itself a powerful learning tool? Sharing your knowledge doesn't just empower those you teach; it reinforces your understanding and challenges you to clarify your thoughts. Education, in this sense, becomes cyclical and social—it's sharing to grow together. It becomes part of your narrative—in mentoring others, you find new insights and solidify your own learnings.

Now, let's also consider another ally of learning—technology. The digital world has revolutionized how we access information. Podcasts, online videos, and interactive courses allow learning to happen anytime, anywhere. Embrace these tools. They're not replacements for traditional learning; rather, they are complements that can enrich your educational journey with flexibility and diversity.

Balance, too, plays a role in lifelong education. There's a temptation to get lost in the pursuit of knowledge—to become a jack-of-all-trades and master of none. Quality is key. It's about deliberate learning. Choose topics that resonate with your passions, professional aspirations, or curiosity. By being selective, you ensure that the time invested in education is time spent wisely, taking you toward your ultimate vision.

Embracing lifelong education also means staying in tune with times and trends. Today's champion must be an adaptable chameleon, constantly evolving in sync with the shifts in society, technology, and industry. Lifelong education keeps your mind sharp, ready to pivot when required, and open to the flow of innovation that characterizes our age.

So how do you go about integrating lifelong education into your everyday life? Start small. Choose one area of interest and dedicate a small portion of your day to learning something about it. Make it a habit, as essential as your morning cup of coffee. Let the seeds of curiosity sprout into routines that tirelessly fuel your growth.

As progress is made, celebrate it! Much like tracking your achievements, keep a learning journal. Write down what you've learned, how you've applied it, and the results you've witnessed. This not only holds you accountable but provides a tangible reflection of your educational journey—a map of how far you've come.

In closing this chapter on lifelong education, remember it's not about the certificates or degrees that hang on your wall. It's about the less tangible but more significant transformation that occurs within you. It's about becoming an individual who is responsive, not reactive; diverse in thought and skill, and forever young at heart, always eager to learn and grow. Embrace the journey of lifelong education, and watch as it transforms you into the champion you are destined to be.

Learning from Diverse Sources

As we've established the importance of lifelong education in staying ahead of the game, one can't stress enough the value brought by learning from diverse sources. The path to enduring wisdom isn't paved by walking a single road; rather, it's an intricate web of multiple pathways, each offering unique experiences and insights. It's time to open our minds and extend our reach when it comes to where and how we learn.

Diversity in learning goes beyond just reading different books or attending various seminars. It means exposing yourself to contrasting viewpoints, embracing different cultures, engaging with individuals who challenge your presuppositions, and constantly searching for the unexpected lessons in everyday life. This practice doesn't merely add to your knowledge base - it broadens your perspective, deepens your understanding, and increases your adaptability.

Let's consider the traditional classroom setting. While it remains a vital environment for learning, can we agree that the world outside those four walls is overflowing with lessons waiting to be discovered? Engaging with experiences you would typically overlook - like a conversation with an elder in a nursing home, or listening to a podcast from a discipline entirely unrelated to your field - can be transformative.

Why is this so? Because the cross-pollination of ideas fuels innovation. It equips you with the ability to connect seemingly unrelated dots, creating solutions that a single-minded focus never could. Each new encounter or idea holds the potential to ignite a spark, driving you towards insights that could revolutionize your understanding of yourself and the world around you.

Think about social media - often branded as a time-waster. However, when utilized with intention, platforms like Twitter, LinkedIn, or even niche online forums can be goldmines for learning. They allow you to follow thought leaders, experts, and trailblazers, observing their thoughts on real-time trends and their approaches to challenges.

Books are undoubtedly a powerful resource for learning. But what about diversifying the authors, genres, and subjects you read? Delving into literature from around the globe enables you to view life through various cultural lenses. Every book is a portal to a different dimension of human experience, every article a window, every documentary a bridge to another aspect of existence.

Workshops and classes outside your expertise can be humbling yet incredibly enriching. Dancing, painting, or coding - these activities demand different skills and thought processes. They teach you to embrace being a novice, to enjoy the process of learning, and to appreciate the journey toward competence in a new realm.

Conversations with strangers often hold unexpectedly profound lessons. Each person you come into contact with is a living library, rich with chapters full of experiences you've never lived. Listening, truly listening, to their stories can transform your understanding in ways that defy the limitations of your individual life story.

Travel, too, is an unmatched teacher. While we'll discuss this in greater depth later, it's worth mentioning now that every trip offers a unique course in geography, sociology, and humility - if we are open to learning. The customs, traditions, and daily lives of others are ripe with lessons on connectivity and humanity.

Volunteering at local organizations provides insight into the struggles and triumphs within your community. It's a practical exercise in empathy and often offers a stark reality check against what you perceive as 'big problems' in life. The struggles and victories of others can offer an education that's not based on theory but on lived experience.

Do not underestimate the role technology plays in expanding your learning sources. Digital courses, virtual reality experiences, and interactive tools can adapt to cater to your learning style, presenting information in innovative ways that traditional methods may not.

It's equally critical to engage with art in all its forms. Whether it's music, cinema, theater, or visual arts, these expressions of human creativity can convey complex ideas, emotions, and narratives that defy straightforward explanation. Engaging with art stimulates different aspects of your brain and can inspire fresh insights.

Let's acknowledge the valuable lessons found in silence. Yes, even in the quiet moments of reflection, meditation, or a stroll through nature, learning happens. These can be the times when the noise of the world falls away, and the voice within you speaks the loudest truths and wisdom.

And when it comes to learning from others, let's not just look up - let's look around. Your peers, younger generations, and those walking a different life path than you can all teach you something valuable. There's wisdom in every stage of life and from every vantage point if you're attentive.

In essence, to learn from diverse sources is to live with a boundless curiosity and an open heart. It's to perceive every encounter as a classroom, and every experience as a rich text to be absorbed. By diversifying your sources of knowledge, you not only enrich your intellect but also your empathy, your adaptability, and your soul. And isn't that the true mark of a champion?

Chapter 19

Mindfulness and Presence

As we pivot from the lifelong quest for knowledge to honing our mental faculties, we arrive at a transformative crossroads: embracing mindfulness and being truly present. It's often in the quietest moments that the loudest victories are won. Imagine the edge you can have when your mind isn't just a sharpened sword, but a tranquil sanctuary, even amidst life's relentless hustle. This isn't about detaching from reality; it's about immersing ourselves so deeply in the here and now that each moment becomes a clear droplet in the pond of our existence. By cultivating a practice grounded in the 'Power of Now,' we unlock our ability to focus, to breathe through chaos, and to act with intention. Meditation isn't just for those seeking spiritual enlightenment—it's a tool, as practical as it is profound, providing mental clarity that cuts through doubt and distraction. If you've ever felt pulled in a million directions, unable to hold onto the fleeting present, breathe ease into that tension. Here, we'll explore how to root ourselves firmly where our power is most potent—in the irreplaceable and unrepeatable present moment.

The Power of Now

The Power of Now isn't just a catchy phrase—it's a transformative concept. It's about seizing this moment that we're in, right here, right now, and recognizing its infinite potential. It's about stepping into the current scene of your life's play and owning your role with conviction.

This moment —yes, this one— is ripe with possibility. Past is a memory. The future is a projection. Now is the real deal. It's what we have in our hands; it's the sculptor's clay, the artist's canvas, the writer's blank page. What you choose to do with it, how far you allow your thoughts to wander, how deeply you engage with your current experience—that defines your power.

To harness the power of now, you must consciously pull yourself back whenever your mind wanders off into yesterday or tasks its binoculars to peer into tomorrow. There's an art to drowning out the buzzing background noise of past and future and tuning in to the clear channel of the present.

Imagine you're an athlete in the blocks, poised for the starting gun. Every ounce of your training, the sweat, and the discipline, it's all led to this now. When the gun goes off, there's no time for second-guessing past workouts or planning the victory party. There's only the now, running the race, one powerful stride at a time. That's living the power of now—it's an athlete in their element, absorbed in the moment.

But let's break it down further. When you focus on the now, you're in the driver's seat of your own consciousness. The chatter that can often lead to anxiety and stress? It fades away when you zero in on what's in front of you. The practice of being present affects not just your mental health, but it influences your physical well-being, your relationships, and your work.

Ever noticed how the most contented and successful individuals have this uncanny ability to remain unflustered in the face of chaos? It's not always natural. Often, it's a learned skill—staying anchored in the now, regardless of life's storms.

It's important to note though, embracing the now doesn't mean you disregard planning for the future or learning from the past. Far from it. It's about finding that delicate balance where memories and ambitions do not overshadow the immediacy of living.

Another facet of the power of now lies in its universality. Whether you're a CEO or a student, a parent or a painter, living in the now is universally relevant. It's about fully immersing yourself in a conversation, savoring a meal, or feeling the burn in each rep at the gym. It's about mindfulness—be it washing dishes or strategizing in the boardroom. Whatever you do, do it with full attention.

When you're present, it shows. People sense it. Your eyes glimmer with intention, your thoughts align with your speech, and your actions follow suit. This kind of congruence is magnetic; it draws people in, it stimulates trust, and it encourages connection. This is as much about interpersonal skills as it is about intrapersonal peace.

Focusing on the now doesn't mean obstacles will cease to exist. But it does equip you with a renewed sense of clarity and composure to navigate them. In the throes of adversity, the now is your haven, a place to gather yourself and respond rather than react.

Consider for a moment the simplest of acts—breathing. You do it without thinking, but what if you brought your attention to it? The inhale fills you, and the exhale releases tension. It's a cycle that's always occurring, but when you're present with it, it becomes a tool for tranquility—a miniature retreat into now.

I challenge you to make small shifts towards the now. When you find your mind rehearsing an upcoming meeting during time with your family, gently remind yourself to come back to now. When you're enjoying a movie, but also scrolling through your phone, choose the movie fully. Small moments. That's where the power builds.

Remember, every champion was once a contender who refused to give up. But more than that, they were someone who refused to be anywhere but in the present moment when it mattered most. They lived and breathed the now with precision and purpose.

So, let's grasp this unwavering truth together: the now is all we've got, and it's where our potential flourishes. It's where fear loses its grip and where joy dances in pure, unadulterated form. It's where you find the strength to keep going, the grace to be grateful, and the fortitude to forge ahead.

Gaze around. This moment—isn't it brimming with life? Isn't it heavy with the stuff of stars, rich with opportunity, echoing with footsteps of the future you're about to walk into? This moment, the now, is your undeniable, unstoppable power.

Meditation for Mental Clarity

As we continue our exploration of well-being in the pursuit of excellence, let's dive deep into the tranquil pool of meditation. This tool isn't just for those seeking spiritual enlightenment but is a practical resource for gaining mental clarity. Why is this simple practice so revolutionary? Well, clarity is to the mind what space is to a crowded room—it allows you to move with ease and purpose.

Meditation is often portrayed as a daunting task requiring years of practice. However, in reality, it's as accessible as the nearest quiet corner. Imagine sitting down after a long day, closing your eyes, and entering a state where your thoughts no longer run rampant. This isn't the domain of mystics; it's an achievable state for anyone willing to take a few minutes each day to practice stillness.

Let's disrupt a common myth: meditation isn't about wiping the mind clean of thoughts. Instead, it's about observing those thoughts without judgment. Think of your mind as a sky and your thoughts as clouds—some days will be overcast, others clear. The goal isn't to banish the clouds but to find peace amidst them, recognizing that just like the sky, the essence of your mind is uncluttered, open, and constantly in a state of calm.

So why meditate? When you meditate, you're training your mind to focus and redirect your thoughts. This practice enhances attention and concentration, which are fundamental for executing goals with precision. Instead of being swept away by a current of distractions, you'll learn to anchor yourself to the moment at hand. And that's where the magic happens.

The benefits of meditation don't end there. Studies have shown that regular meditation can reduce stress, control anxiety, promote emotional health, and enhance self-awareness. These perks contribute to a mental environment where clarity thrives. It's like upgrading your mental operating system to handle life's challenges with greater ease.

If you're concerned about the time investment, think about it as allocating resources to improve your overall performance. Just like a car needs regular oil changes to run smoothly, your mind needs moments of stillness to operate at peak performance. Meditation isn't a luxury; it's maintenance for the mind.

And what about those times when negativity seems to cloud your vision? Meditation introduces you to mindfulness, a way to acknowledge and accept your thoughts and feelings without letting them dictate your actions. It's an effective tool for silencing that inner critic who loves to chant tales of self-doubt and fear.

Getting started with meditation can be as simple as finding a comfortable seat, setting a timer for a few minutes, and focusing on your breath. That's right, just breathe. Inhale. Exhale. Follow the rhythm. When your mind wanders—as it will—gently guide it back to your breath. This simple act is like lifting weights for your brain, growing stronger with each session.

As your practice deepens, you may want to explore different types of meditation. Maybe you'll resonate with guided meditations, where a calm voice leads you through visualizations or mantras. Possibly, you'll find solace in movement-based practices, like walking meditations, where the rhythm of your steps becomes your focus.

Remember that while meditation promotes mental clarity, it's also about building a better relationship with yourself. It's self-care on a fundamental level. Honoring the time you set aside for meditation is like saying, "Yes, I'm worth it. Yes, I can give this gift to myself."

For skeptics still on the fence, give it a try. What have you got to lose, apart from a few minutes that might have been spent scrolling through your phone? It's a low investment with a potentially high return on clarity, focus, and emotional resilience.

As you build your meditation practice, consider how it aligns with your goals and vision from earlier chapters. What would greater mental clarity mean for your ambitions? How could heightened focus and reduced anxiety transform your approach to challenges? These aren't abstract benefits; they are practical tools you can use to navigate your path to success.

Taking a moment to meditate is not retreating from the world—it's preparing to engage with it more fully. It's like sharpening a knife; the process isn't the end goal, but a sharp knife cuts through tasks with far more ease than a dull one. Similarly, a clear mind slices through life's complexities and reveals solutions with far more precision.

Ultimately, meditation for mental clarity is about investing in your most valuable asset—your mind. In this fast-paced, demanding world, granting yourself the clarity that comes from meditation could be the ace up your sleeve, the secret sauce that distinguishes a life of chaos from a life of triumph. Embrace the stillness, harness the clarity, and watch as your path to victory becomes a journey of purposeful steps rather than a tiring sprint.

Let's not dismiss meditation as a mere trend or fad; it's a timeless practice that has refined the minds of countless individuals who have shaped the world. The champions of old knew this secret, and now, so do you. Infuse this practice into your life, and witness the transformation not just in your mindset, but in the quality of your life's tapestry.

FAYE DONOVAN

Chapter 20

Recognizing and Celebrating Your Wins

As our journey brings us to a much-needed moment of reflection, it's essential we take a step back to bask in the victories we've achieved, no matter the size. You've been grinding, setting your intentions day after day, and now, we're here—ready to honor each milestone reached on this path to self-improvement and empowerment. Let's face it: you've been pushing yourself, constantly chasing the next peak, but have you truly allowed yourself to savor the view from the summits you've conquered? It's not just about acknowledging your accomplishments; it's about immersing in that sweet spot of joy that comes with knowing you've outdone yourself. By tracking your trajectory, you position yourself to see just how far you've come—this isn't vanity; it's an absolute necessity for maintaining momentum. And when it comes to rewarding your grit and passion, throw away the notion that it's self-indulgent. Celebrating what you've achieved is a signal to your mind and soul that the struggle is worth it, that the finish line isn't just a mark of completion, but a herald of the new beginnings and endless possibilities that await. So pause, raise a glass, share your victories, and let that satisfaction seep deeply into your bones. It fuels the fire for tomorrow's victories, and trust me, those are just around the bend.

Tracking Progress

Tracking progress brings to light that captivating sense of victory at every milestone. It's the heartbeat of our journey towards self-improvement, a tool so essential yet often overlooked. Picture this - you've got your eyes on the prize, a plan in hand, and an unyielding spirit. But how do you make sure you're not just running in place?

Imagine tracking progress as setting up signposts on your path. These signposts are there to celebrate, to reflect, and even to recalibrate. They're not just indicators of where you are; they speak volumes about how far you've come. It's like giving yourself a high-five, a nod that you are indeed moving forward.

Start simple. Journals aren't just for poets or starry-eyed dreamers; they are a winner's secret weapon. Documenting your journey provides a tangible timeline of triumphs and trials. On days when motivation seems like a distant memory, these pages will remind you that yes, progress has been made.

And let's talk about goals. Break them down – macro, micro, you name it. When you dissect a larger goal into bite-sized pieces, tracking progress becomes a lot less daunting. Each small success is a building block, a steady climb up the mountain of your grand vision.

But how can we make these intangible attributes of progress concrete? Metrics. They come in all shapes and sizes, but they must resonate with your specific goals. Whether it's a numeric value, a feeling, or a level of mastery, define what progress looks like to you. Then, measure it, chronicle it, and yes, flaunt it. But always with the delicate balance of humility and pride.

In the grand scheme of things, feedback loops are your friends. It might sound technical, but it's just a fancy way of saying: Action. Feedback. Improvement. Repeat. This cycle propels you like a slingshot further and further with each iteration. Feedback loops can present themselves in a myriad of ways: a weekly review, a monthly sit-down, or even an impromptu self-check-in.

Don't shy away from technology. There's an app for literally everything these days. Leveraging these digital tools can help automate the tracking process, giving you more time to focus on the doing rather than the documenting. Plus, they often come with shiny graphs and motivating alerts to keep you hooked on your progress.

But tracking isn't always about the sunshine and rainbows of success. It's crucial to document the downpours too. By recording the lows with the highs, you build a reservoir of lessons learned. It's honest tracking that paves the road to resilience and real, sustainable progress.

A dash of creativity can also spice up tracking. Vision boards, progress bars, color-coded spreadsheets – choose what enlivens your spirit. Turning the mundane into a visual festival can inject that much-needed whimsy and wonder into the day-to-day grind.

Then there's the community aspect. Sharing progress milestones with a trusted group or mentor can amplify your commitment to your goals. It brings a sense of accountability that could be the very catalyst needed for those quantum leaps in personal growth.

Stagnation is a sneaky thief of potential. By setting check-in points, you create an antidote to complacency. It's about kindling the fires of ambition regularly and refusing to let the flame falter. These checkpoints act as prompts, propelling you to ask, "Am I closer to where I wish to be?"

Don't forget – celebrate the wins, no matter how small. There's no victory too insignificant in the autobiography of your success. These celebrations are reminders that the journey, with all its ebbs and flows, is just as valuable as the destination. They imbue your travels with joy, the kind that fuels the soul.

When you do hit a plateau, tracking progress becomes a beacon that guides adjustments. It answers the vital questions – Where did I veer off? What can I tweak? Then, armed with these insights, you evolve strategies, making your climb smarter, not just harder.

In essence, tracking progress is a mirror reflecting the true face of your endeavor. It's unbiased, unforgiving, and at times, an incredibly fulfilling snapshot of your transformation. It's this consistent and honest appraisal that stitches the fragments of effort into a quilt of experience, wisdom, and ultimately, triumph.

Remember, the act of tracking is not just about etching ticks on a wall. It's about the awareness it fosters – a mindfulness of movement and growth. It keeps you grounded yet allows your dreams the runway to take flight. So go ahead, take that diligent step, and mark your journey, for each tick is a testament to your indomitable spirit and your relentless pursuit of excellence.

Rewarding Effort and Achievement

Rewarding Effort and Achievement paints the picture of truly recognizing the milestones you've reached and the immense work you've put in so far. It's a vital piece of the puzzle for building lasting motivation, and it's through this lens we'll delve deeper.

First, let's get one thing straight: while it's critical to keep your eyes on the prize, it's equally important to value the blood, sweat, and tears you pour into the journey. Consider for a moment the last time you really patted yourself on the back. Felt good, didn't it? Now imagine weaving that same recognition into your routine more regularly.

You see, the thing about effort is that it's the one thing totally within your control. Outcomes? They can be fickle, subject to a hundred external variables, but effort, that's all you need. Rewarding that effort is acknowledging the power you have to impact your path, regardless of the outcome. It's a celebration of the agency you wield on a daily basis.

But how do we go about it? It's not just about grand gestures—it's about creating a sustainable practice of recognition that fuels your fire. Here's an idea: create a 'win log', a simple document, or a note on your phone, and jot down daily efforts that moved the needle, no matter how small. Review these regularly and bask in the glory of your unwavering commitment.

This practice does something quite powerful. It shifts your mindset from a pure results-based trajectory to a journey-minded approach. It's not just about the trophies and accolades—though they're nice—it's about the person you're becoming on your way there: someone who values perseverance and dedication.

Let's pivot slightly and talk about achievement. Once you've hit a milestone, what's next? Do you take a moment to celebrate it, or are you immediately onto the next thing? Here's where a lot of driven individuals trip up. Without pausing to really soak in a success, it's easy to burn out. That's why it's crucial to create a ritual around celebrating achievements.

What that celebration looks like is personal. Maybe it's a special meal, an afternoon off, or a social media post that lets your circle cheer you on. Whatever it is, make it significant enough that it registers as a genuine reward for your hard work.

Now, let's loop in those around us. It can be transformative to share celebrations with friends, family, or even colleagues. When they recognize your achievements, it doesn't just magnify the joy—it also cements your victories in the narrative of your life. They become not just personal triumphs but shared chapters in your story.

Beyond the personal, let's think bigger picture. How does a company or organization flourish? Often, it's a culture that rewards not just results but the innovative attempts, regardless of their outcome. Likewise, you should appraise your own ventures with this lens. Did your attempt not pan out? No problem—if the approach was commendable, that's worthy of recognition too.

Granted, you won't always get external validation—you don't control the reactions of others, after all. But you can control your own, and by adopting a self-celebratory habit, you're less dependent on external praise to feel a sense of accomplishment.

Ever heard of a victory lap? It's that extra run around the track you take after a win. You can apply this concept to your life: after an accomplishment, take time to indulge in activities that recharge you and provide a mental 'lap' to relish in what you've done. This isn't wasted time—think of it as investing in your morale bank.

All this talk about rewards has an undertone, though: balance. Rewarding yourself shouldn't sink your ship; it should be fuel to keep it sailing. So, the key is to match the reward to the size of the achievement. Finished a week-long project? Maybe a nice evening out is in order. Wrapped up a year-long endeavor? That might call for something more substantial, like a weekend getaway.

Education often fails to teach us about the art of self-acknowledgment. Remember that you're not just a human doing; you're a human being. And being proud of your efforts and achievements is a healthy part of existence. It's not about ego; it's about recognizing the journey of growth you're on.

Cultivate the habit of asking yourself at the end of each day, "What did I do well today?" It's a simple question, but it can have profound effects on your self-esteem and motivation. By focusing on effort as well as success, you're building a foundation of positive reinforcement that can see you through challenges and spur you on to greater heights.

In wrapping up, it's crucial to emphasize that rewarding effort and achievement is not a one-time thing. Make it part of your culture, your personal policy. It's an evolving practice that changes as you grow but remains a cornerstone of a fulfilling journey to victory. Keep celebrating the steps you take, and you'll find yourself not just aiming for success but also enjoying the rich, rewarding path to getting there.

Chapter 21

Handling Criticism and Feedback

As we journey from recognizing our triumphs, we naturally encounter moments where the world serves us a slice of humble pie through criticism and feedback. It's easy to shine when praise lights our path, but the true test of our mettle is not just in how we bask in applause, but how we stand firm and grow when faced with critique. Let's think of feedback—not as arrows aimed to wound—but as seeds planted by others that, if tended with care, can grow into our greatest strengths. We all need a sounding board to echo back the truths we can't see ourselves; however, it's vital to discern which echoes to amplify and which to let fade. When feedback comes knocking, let's swing that door wide open with an open heart and a keen mind, ready to sift through the words for nuggets of wisdom that can propel us even closer to our pinnacle of potential. So take it in, reflect, and harness the power of perspectives outside your own. After all, a champion is sculpted by many hands, some guiding and others challenging, but each shaping you into your finest form.

Constructive vs. Destructive Feedback

Imagine stepping off the stage after giving what felt like a keynote speech for the ages. Your palms still echoing the resonance of the microphone, your heart still riding the high of applause. Now, as the curtain falls, someone approaches you with feedback. The words they choose, the intent behind them, and the way they're delivered has the power to either elevate your spirits or crush them beneath the weight of criticism. This is where we draw the line between constructive and destructive feedback. This line profoundly impacts our journey towards becoming the best we can be.

Constructive feedback is a cornerstone in the foundation of growth. It's delivered with a keen sense of awareness and empathy, mindful of the fact that its ultimate goal is to nurture progress, not hinder it. When you receive constructive feedback, it feels like someone is walking beside you with a torch when you're navigating through an otherwise unforgiving tunnel. It's specific, actionable, and suffused with a clear intention of helping you do better next time.

On the flip side, destructive feedback crashes into your world like an uninvited storm, wreaking havoc with its aimless or ill-intentioned criticism. It tends to be vague, rooted in negative emotions, and often leaves you with feelings of deflation rather than inspiration. It's the kind of critique that offers no foothold for improvement, serving more as a reflection of the speaker's own limitations rather than a constructive commentary on your performance.

Now, let's talk about the art of discerning constructive feedback from its counterpart. It's absolutely critical to distinguish which type you're receiving. Constructive feedback typically comes from those who have a stake in your growth and success. These individuals care enough to take the time to provide detailed insights and are usually open to a dialogue. They do not just point out what went wrong; they also shine a spotlight on what went right and frame suggestions in a positive, growth-oriented way.

In the game of life, especially when you're striving for excellence, it's central to seek out those who can offer you the former type of feedback. They are the mentors, the supportive colleagues, and thoughtful friends who become part of your team, your personal board of advisors, if you will. Their words are fuel to your fire, not water dampening your spirit.

It's also worth noting that how we receive and process feedback is equally important to our development. Embrace the mindset of a student, always open to learning. When faced with feedback, filter it through a lens of objectivity and ask yourself, "What can I learn from this?" It's a question that turns even the toughest feedback into a stepping stone on your path to success.

Remember, we all have blind spots and areas where we can't see the full picture. Constructive feedback acts like a mirror, revealing those parts of our performance that we're too close to see clearly. It offers us an outside perspective that, when reflected upon with an open and curious mind, can lead to powerful insights and change.

Meanwhile, when confronted with destructive feedback, the key is not to erect walls around your self-esteem but to maintain a healthy boundary between critique and your sense of self-worth. Acknowledge the comment, consider the source, and then decide if there's any small kernel of truth that you can extract and use to your advantage. If not, let it go as effortlessly as leaves falling from a tree – natural and unburdening.

Adopting this selective filtering of feedback is not just about protecting your morale; it's about consciously choosing the influences that shape your journey. You have the power to decide who gets a seat at your table of progress and who has the privilege of offering insights that can recalibrate your trajectory towards winning.

Engaging in active listening is vital when receiving feedback. This doesn't mean merely hearing the words but understanding the message behind them. It's about responding with poise and grace, not defensiveness. By doing so, you ensure that the exchange is a dialogue, not a monologue, giving you a voice in your development process and making sure the conversation remains productive.

Moreover, giving constructive feedback is just as much an acquired skill as receiving it. When you're in a position to offer guidance, do so with the clarity, purpose, and kindness of a true leader. Be specific. Be helpful. Illuminate the path forward instead of simply showcasing the stumbling blocks. After all, the manner in which you convey your thoughts can either uplift someone to reach new heights or inadvertently clip their wings.

As you walk through life's myriad corridors of achievement and challenge, keep in mind that feedback is an omnipresent force. It can either be your ally or your adversary. It is an instrument of communication that, when tuned just right, harmonizes with your aspirations, pushing you to newer, grander symphonies of success.

So, whether you're on the giving or receiving end of feedback, approach it with reverence for its power. Engage with it as a tool that sharpens, shapes, and refines. And most importantly, recognize that in every piece of feedback lies the potential for transformation – for it's in those moments of exchange that the seeds of a champion are nurtured.

The balance between offering and accepting feedback is a subtle dance that can propel you forward or keep you standing still. Striking the right chord not only fortifies you against setbacks but also empowers you to reach for higher levels of achievement. Engage with feedback as you would a skilled sparring partner in the ring – with respect, strategy, and the wisdom to know that each interaction makes you stronger and brings you closer to victory.

Remember, the path to being a champion is paved with countless moments of learning. Constructive feedback is your compass on this journey; it points you in the direction of growth, excellence, and, ultimately, triumph. So, as you absorb the insights from those invested in your success, you're not only refining your skills but also enhancing your capacity to rise to life's challenges as a true champion would.

Growing from Others' Perspectives

Growing from Others' Perspectives is a crucial step on the pathway to personal growth and success. Every person we encounter has a distinct lens through which they see the world, informed by their experiences, culture, and knowledge. Unearthing the rare gems in these myriad perspectives can be an enlightening voyage, one that expands our understanding and enhances our wisdom. Let's dive into the wealth of growth that can be found in embracing the viewpoints of those around us.

Imagine a mosaic, a stunning piece of art consisting of numerous small, colored pieces of glass or stone. Each fragment alone is beautiful, yet when combined, they create a masterpiece of greater significance and splendor. This is the power of collective insight from diverse perspectives. When we actively seek to understand where others are coming from, we not only cultivate empathy but also benefit from a broader scope of knowledge that can propel us toward our goals.

Often, we find ourselves enveloped in our personal bubbles, comfortable with what we know and resistant to what challenges our status quo. This comfort zone, however, becomes a barrier to innovation and growth. When we open up to the views of others, especially those who differ from us, we challenge our preconceptions and discover new ways of thinking. These revelations are the catalysts for innovation, the fuel that drives us toward excellence.

To effectively tap into the perspectives of others, active listening is key. It's easy to listen with the intent to reply, formulating our response while the other person is still speaking. However, the art of listening lies in truly hearing - comprehending the depth of what's being shared without judgment or the rush to respond. It's in those moments of true attentiveness that wisdom is shared and received.

It's not just the content of what is said that matters but the context in which it's delivered. Looking beyond words and understanding the emotions and experiences behind them enriches our comprehension. This depth of insight helps us adapt our approach both in life and in our interactions, fostering more meaningful connections and strategies.

Much like a gardener learns from the environment to cultivate different plants, we too must tend to the various perspectives we encounter. Questions such as, "What can I learn from this viewpoint?" or "How can this insight improve my approach?" transform encounters from mere conversations to learning opportunities.

Collaboration is another fertile ground for growth. Working alongside individuals with different skill sets, backgrounds, and ideas can lead to a higher level of creativity and problem-solving. It's in the melding of minds that solutions to complex problems are often unearthed.

Feedback, both positive and critical, is a gift from another's perspective. Positive feedback reinforces our strengths, while constructive criticism shines a light on areas for improvement. Embrace both with gratitude, for they are tools that hone our talents and abilities.

Such growth, however, isn't without its discomfort. At times, integrating others' perspectives into our growth journey can surface internal resistance. It's only by working through this discomfort that we form new, stronger mindsets primed for progress.

Equally important is discernment. Not all advice or perspectives will align with our path, and that's okay. Sifting through the cacophony of voices to find those that resonate with our inner truth is an invaluable skill. It's not about adopting every viewpoint, but rather finding harmony between external insight and internal wisdom.

Understanding diverse cultures and societies also plays a role in broadening our perspectives. Exposure to different ways of life augments our worldview, fostering adaptability and the ability to navigate the globalized world with finesse.

Incorporating the perspectives of others into our lives doesn't mean losing our sense of self. It's quite the opposite; it allows us to build a robust foundation of identity, firm in our beliefs yet flexible in our approach, equipped to manage the ebbs and flows of life more gracefully.

Remember that our individual journeys are interlaced with countless others, each with their own wealth of knowledge and experience. As we interconnect, we begin to see how the threads of our lives weave into a larger, more beautiful tapestry of human experience.

To conclude, thriving in the diversity of thought and experience is akin to nurturing a garden in full bloom. It takes patience, willingness, and a love for learning. But when the time comes to harvest, the fruits borne from the seeds of others' perspectives are not only bountiful; they are life-changing.

As we progress in our personal and professional lives, let us do so with open arms, ready to welcome and grow from the fertile ground of others' perspectives. They say a wise person learns from their own mistakes, but a wiser one learns from the mistakes of others. Perhaps the wisest of all is the one who learns not just from the missteps but also from the insights, experiences, and wisdom that others are ready to share. Let's be that wise one, constantly evolving, constantly growing, and on the constant lookout for the myriad of perspectives that can shape us into champions.

Chapter 22

Sustainable Success

As we shift our focus towards a kind of victory that's meant to last, we dive into the heart of *Sustainable Success*. It's one thing to sprint towards a finish line buoyed by adrenaline; it's entirely another to cultivate success that grows and adapts with you over your lifetime. Imagine a garden that isn't just planted with enthusiasm but is tended to day after day, with patience and foresight—where the fruits of labor are not merely consumed but replanted for the next season. That's what we're aiming for. The success that is responsible, that considers the environmental impact, the personal growth, and the community connection in its stride, is a success that doesn't fade when trends shift, or circumstances change. Here, we explore the roots of your ambitions, and much like a sapling nurtured into a towering tree, we discuss how consistency, adaptability, and communal ethos merged with your vision can create a legacy of triumph that outlasts the ebb and flow of fortune.

Long-Term Visioning

It's the guiding star, the distant lighthouse that keeps your ship steering through the darkest nights and the stormiest seas. Having a long-term vision is like planting a tree you might never sit under; it's the belief in a future you're shaping with every choice you make today. So, what's your grand vision? Take a moment. Really picture it. See yourself in that snapshot of the future, where your consistent efforts have bloomed into the success you're actively pursuing.

Now let's talk practicality. When you're immersed in your day-to-day hustle, it can be easy to lose sight of where you're heading. That's precisely why long-term visioning matters. It pulls you back from the brink of short-term gratification and keeps you anchored to what truly counts. Dreaming big isn't just for the young or the idealistic; it's for the doers, the strategists, the ones who understand that every empire was once an idea someone refused to give up on.

Creating a vivid and compelling long-term vision involves a mix of imagination, clarity, and ambition. Start by asking yourself: Where do I want to be in 10, 20, or even 30 years? Who's with me? How am I impacting the world? Once you begin decoding these mysteries, you start turning the intangible into actionable blueprints for the journey ahead.

But here's where most people stumble. They confuse a long-term vision with a rigid plan set in stone. Life has a funny way of throwing curveballs, and your vision needs to be both resilient and flexible. Think of it as setting your GPS for a cross-country road trip. You know your destination, but you're open to different paths that may get you there, some sights you didn't plan to see, and lessons you learn along the way.

Fleshing out your long-term vision is more than just personal. It's also about how you see yourself contributing to the greater good. What legacy are you leaving behind? What stories will be told about you? Consider the ripple effects of your actions, how they touch lives, shift paradigms, and elevate those around you.

Now, let's break down this grand vision into more digestible chunks. This is where your mid-term goals come into play. Think of these as milestones or checkpoints that keep you aligned with the bigger picture. If your vision is the book you're writing, these goals are the chapters that make it a story worth reading. They should be significant enough to challenge you, but not so daunting that they leave you disheartened.

Cultivate patience. Remember, a long-term vision is not a quick fix. It's a commitment to a process of transformation, and processes take time. Sometimes, it'll feel like you're moving at a snail's pace, but as long as you're moving forward, you're still in the race. Patience means giving yourself room to grow and learn without the pressure of immediacy dampening your spirit.

To stay on track with your vision:

1. Revisit it often.

2. Keep it fresh in your mind.

3. Make it a ritual to visualize where you want to be, to feel it in your bones.

This isn't about obsessing – it's about staying connected to the why behind the grind. It's the fuel when your tank is empty, the comfort when doubt creeps in.

As you envision this long-term future, think about the skills you'll need to master, the knowledge you'll have to acquire, and the network you'll have to build. No hero's journey is devoid of guides, mentors, and allies. Your personal development is a critical part of your long-term planning. Be willing to learn and grow.

Prepare for setbacks. They're par for the course. When aiming for targets years away, you're bound to encounter many unforeseen challenges. Instead of letting them derail you, use them as an opportunity to adjust your sails, to strengthen your resolve, and to gather stories worth telling when you finally reach your destination.

And while you're charging towards your future, don't forget to appreciate the present moment. Mindfulness is key. The journey towards a long-term vision is made up of 'todays' spent well. Ground yourself in gratitude for where you are and what you have now, even as you strive for what's ahead. This balance is essential to a fulfilling journey.

Moreover, bring others along for your ride. Share your vision. Collaborate. Co-create. Building relationships and communities aligned with your long-term aspirations not only enriches your experience but also amplifies the impact of your efforts. Our interconnectedness is a powerful catalyst for change, both personal and global.

In the end, your long-term vision is a living entity. It's subject to evolution as you grow, discover, and refine what truly matters to you. Flexibility in approach does not equal a lack of commitment; it's wisdom in action. Be ready to adapt your vision as life unfolds, as you gather new information, as you soar to new heights.

Nurture your vision as you would a garden, with attention, care, and love, knowing that in time it will bear fruit. Savor the process, the daily acts of courage, the discipline, the persistence. Your long-term vision is not just a destination; it's a testament to the life you choose to lead every single day, starting from this moment on.

So keep your eyes on the horizon, your hands on the work that matters, and your heart in the game. The future you're dreaming of is crafted by the decisions you make right now. Let your long-term vision be the compass that guides you through life's complexities, knowing that each step you take is a step towards a legacy of greatness you alone can build.

Environmental Awareness in Your Journey

As you cultivate the drive and determination to chase down your victories and etch your name in the annals of those who dare to reach higher, it's crucial to acknowledge a silent partner in your quest – the environment. Your journey towards self-improvement and achievement does not unfold in a vacuum; rather, it's woven into the tapestry of our shared environment, which is why its protection should seamlessly join the ranks of our ambitions.

Consider this: the spaces we occupy, the air we breathe, and the resources we consume all play a vital role in shaping our well-being, which in turn affects our capacity to focus, persevere, and triumph. Tuning into the environmental consequences of our actions fosters not only personal growth but also a robust consciousness that helps us thrive within the nexus of nature and human ambition.

We often drown in the noise of ambition and forget that silence and harmony with nature are where insights are born. The successful individuals of tomorrow are those who learn to draw strength from the calm whispers of nature while contributing positively to its narrative. Picture this – a world where each of us moves with a careful tread, always aware of the footprint we leave behind. Isn't that the mark of a true champion?

Thinking green doesn't just benefit the planet; it refines your character. It means living with intention, practicing restraint when necessary, and making choices that reflect not just self-interest but a greater good. It's about understanding the ripple effect of our actions, as each drop of effort contributes to a tide of change. Success, then, becomes a shared victory, not just for us but for the world that sustains us.

Integrating sustainability into your goals isn't just morally astute; it's pragmatic. Companies across the globe are recognizing that sustainability is not a buzzword but a business imperative. As a forward-thinking individual, aligning your personal brand with environmental stewardship isn't just good for the Earth – it's a competitive edge, a statement that you understand and are prepared for the future landscape of success.

There's power in small, consistent acts of environmental kindness. Opt for a bike ride instead of a car trip, a paperless approach instead of printing reams of documents, or support businesses that commit to sustainable practices. These choices don't just minimize your impact on the planet; they amplify the quality of your victories, ensuring they're not pyrrhic but enduring.

Remember, technology can be a double-edged sword. It's integral to advancement, yet we must wield it wisely. Embrace innovation that conserves resources, like virtual meetings that save travel emissions or cloud storage that diminishes the need for physical servers. By intertwining technology and eco-consciousness, you'll be at the forefront, leading the charge towards a greener future without sacrificing progress.

Challenge the traditional benchmarks of success. The size of your house, the make of your car, and the grandeur of material possessions pale in comparison to the legacy of a healthier planet. Redefining success to include eco-friendly objectives infuses your journey with depth, making your story one of inspiration and aspiration against the backdrop of a larger purpose.

Just as your journey involves a healthy body and a focused mind, it equally demands a vibrant and thriving environment. Exercise outdoors, and meditate in natural settings. You'll find that your quest for personal excellence is enlivened by the life force of the environment. The interdependence between personal health and the Earth's well-being cannot be overstated.

Revisit the chapter on daily habits and routines. Now, imagine integrating green habits into that structure. This is not about grand gestures but incremental changes. Each time you opt for a reusable water bottle, recycle diligently, or choose local produce, you carve a niche of responsibility into your daily life. These practices speak volumes about who you are – an individual who commands respect not just for achievement but for the conscientious path taken to reach there.

As a community, we rise by lifting others, and as global citizens, we thrive by nurturing our planet. Engage with community initiatives focused on environmental conservation. Offer your time, resources, or voice to causes that endeavor to protect our shared home. Through active participation, we weave a thread of collective responsibility into our personal tapestry of growth.

You'll discover, if not already, that financial fitness includes investing in green solutions. Funds, stocks, and bonds that support renewable energies and sustainable practices aren't just ethical plays; they're smart strategies. Forward-thinking investors know that sustainable investments can outperform their traditional counterparts, proving that what's good for the environment can be great for your wallet too.

It's tempting to race towards the finish line, but achieving sustainable success is not a frantic sprint – it's a considered journey. It's a balance of speed and sustainability, of ambition and responsibility. Every choice made with environmental awareness is a step forward, not just for you, but for a world eagerly waiting for champions of both personal success and planetary well-being.

As you turn the pages of this chapter and reflect on the expansive horizon of your wins, let's not overlook the bedrock upon which they're built. Environmental awareness in your journey is not an optional side path; it's a bridge to a future where success is as green as it is golden. There's a regal beauty in striving for greatness while holding hands with nature, ensuring that as you climb, you do not pull the roots of the very ground that upholds you.

Your journey's narrative will have many highlights – achievements, milestones, and ovations. As you pen each chapter with purpose and passion, let the subtext of your actions resonate with an unwavering commitment to the planet. Turn the tide. Be the champion who fought for victories with a vigilant eye on sustainability. After all, in the purest sense, we only triumph when we rise together, with our environment as our most treasured teammate.

Chapter 23

The Ethics of Winning

Stepping out from the shadows of sustainable success, we navigate the crucial terrain of ethics in Chapter 23. Imagine winning that feels hollow, devoid of the rich satisfaction one expects—it's the scenario when success is achieved without a moral compass. Here, our focus is on the wholesome glory found at the intersection of ambition and integrity. It's about understanding that the true measure of our triumphs isn't just the outcome but the character we exhibit in pursuit of those victories. Embracing fair play isn't a detriment to our desire to win; it's the very foundation that ensures the wins are worth celebrating. When we talk about social responsibility, we're acknowledging that our successes have ripple effects, influencing the framework of our communities. Living in an age where every move is scrutinized, holding tight to our principles is non-negotiable. It's the epitome of winning truly, where what you gain isn't just for self-gratification but a testament of honor for all to see—and that's a legacy that outlasts trophies and titles.

Fair Play and Integrity

As we delve into what furnishes the foundation for enduring success, let's shine a spotlight on fair play and integrity. It's the ethical bedrock that supports not just personal victory, but also inspires respect and admiration from cohorts and competitors alike. Walking the path with integrity means aligning your actions with your values, ensuring that every step you take towards success doesn't compromise the person you aspire to be.

Imagine someone at a crossroads, where one path veers into a shadowy shortcut littered with deceit and dishonesty. At the same time, the other follows a more arduous but sunlit route of ethical choices. Opting for the latter, despite its challenges, is what sets apart a true champion. Success achieved without integrity is like a trophy filled with emptiness. Still, when you earn that accolade with your principles intact, it's a reservoir brimming with self-respect and the esteem of your peers.

Fair play isn't just about abiding by the rules of a game; it's about applying an equitable mindset to every aspect of life. From how you interact with colleagues to the transparency you bring to your work, fair play means operating from a place of honesty and respect for others. It's an unwavering commitment to treating others as you would like to be treated, thereby establishing a level playing field for everyone involved.

Reflect on the role models that have left a mark on your life. What threads their legacies together? Isn't it their steadfast adherence to integrity that helps their names endure in the halls of respect? Embodying fair play means you become that role model for others, someone who demonstrates that success is sweetest when it's spiced with morality.

Understand that integrity is your inner compass, guiding you through the stormy seas of temptation and shortcuts. It offers you a clear direction when options are muddied by the disorder of easy wins. Staying true to this compass might be a test when the harsh winds of competition beat against your resolve. Still, the sense of self that remains unshaken in these storms is far more rewarding than any transient victory.

When confronted with ethical dilemmas, take a moment to ponder the eventual repercussions of your decisions. Actions taken in haste can cast long shadows. Still, decisions made with consideration for fairness and integrity illuminate your narrative with a radiant glow. The trust you cultivate through ethical actions is not easily eroded and can become one of your most valuable assets.

It's vital to grasp that integrity is not just a singular act; it's a habit, a continual choice that becomes the very fabric of your life. It's choosing the harder right over the easier wrong, not once, but every time the situation arises. Cultivating this habit means that even in moments of high pressure, your default mode of operation is wired towards ethical behavior.

Dive into your interactions and scrutinize the genuineness of your engagements. Are you lifting others up, or are your actions self-serving at their expense? True champions understand that success can and should be shared. The foundation of long-lasting relationships is mutual growth, rooted in a culture of integrity and collective effort.

Integrity embodies the promise you make to yourself to maintain your morals, even when no one is watching. It's the internal accountability system that checks you, that refuses to let you compromise your values for fleeting gains. This inner auditor codifies your every decision, ensuring that you can look back on your journey without regret.

Embed this philosophy in every goal you chase. When your vision of success is infused with integrity, your aspirations rise higher and become about more than just personal gain. They become a force that can drive positive change in your community and, perhaps, even the world. Triumph interlaced with integrity resonates across the fabric of society and echoes through generations.

Remember, maintaining fair play and integrity might sometimes mean that you forego immediate rewards, yet what you reap in return is credibility. Credibility draws people to you, opens doors that no amount of cunning could, and lays down a red carpet for opportunities that align with your deeply held values.

In the heat of competition, never lose sight of the fact that how you achieve your goals is just as important as the accomplishments themselves. Winning the right way leaves a legacy that transcends the shelves of trophies, the digits in the bank account, or the accolades. It's about being able to carry the weight of your achievements with the lightness of heart that comes from knowing they were earned with integrity.

Finally, let's not forget that fair play and integrity should also pilot your internal dialogue. The way you talk to yourself, the promises you make and keep, and the standards you set for your personal conduct all play into your self-concept. Upholding these values within yourself fertilizes the soil of your psyche in which the seeds of external success are sown.

Forge ahead with the assurance that while the road of integrity may have its share of obstacles, it leads you to a summit where the view is unobstructed by the fog of deceit. The air here is crisp with the rewards of self-respect, mutual respect, and the honor of knowing that you didn't just aim to win; you aimed to win rightly. Fair play and integrity are, intrinsically, the heartbeat of a triumph that is true and timeless.

Social Responsibility

Amidst the dynamic and often self-centric journey toward personal achievement, we come upon an impactful milestone – the concept of social responsibility. It's the intersection where our potential to be a positive force reaches beyond our personal goals and touches the fabric of society. So, let's lean in and explore what it means to be socially responsible and how it strengthens our ascent toward greatness.

Putting it simply, social responsibility is about acknowledging that we're all part of a larger community, and our actions resonate on a wider scale. Each choice we make, every ripple we send out, contributes to the collective experience. When we center some of our efforts on the greater good, we don't just elevate ourselves; we elevate humanity.

Consider this for a moment: the energy and dedication you pour into realizing your dreams have immense power. Now, imagine directing a fraction of that zeal towards societal challenges—be that supporting educational programs, championing for equal rights, or working towards sustainable practices. The impact could be profound, far-reaching, and, ultimately, part of your legacy.

Engaging in community service is one of the most straightforward ways to practice social responsibility. It's direct, hands-on, and often connects you with the very people you're helping. This can manifest as volunteering at local shelters, organizing charitable events, or mentoring the less fortunate. Through service, you don't just give back—you're gifted with perspective, gratitude, and a heart that grows in empathy and understanding.

Philanthropy steps into the realm of more significant financial contributions or fundraising efforts for causes that resonate with your values.

True, not everyone has the same financial means, but philanthropy isn't reserved for the ultra-wealthy. A small, regular donation to a nonprofit, or rallying friends and family to support a cause, are acts that aggregate into substantial assistance.

Furthermore, it's essential to recognize the power of conscious consumerism, which is the practice of purchasing products and supporting companies that are ethical and environmentally responsible. By being intentional with where we spend our money, we can influence industries to operate more sustainably and humanely. It's a simple strategy: support the world you want to live in.

In the business sphere, corporate social responsibility, or CSR, is an expanding realm where companies balance profit-making with beneficial practices for society. As a professional, advocate for your workplace to adopt CSR initiatives. Encourage green practices, diversity and inclusion, and community engagement. Lead by example and influence change from within.

Moving onto environmental stewardship, it's no secret that a healthy planet is crucial for a thriving humanity. Whether you're an individual or a business leader, promoting and engaging in sustainable practices is a responsibility we all share. Make changes to reduce your carbon footprint, stand up against pollution, and champion renewable energy sources. Remember, preserving our planet is akin to safeguarding the future.

Equality and justice are pillars of a harmonious society. Being socially responsible means advocating for those marginalized and discriminated against. Why not harness your potential to be a beacon of change? Engage in dialogues, support policies that promote fairness, and actively participate in making our society more inclusive for all.

Education is the bedrock upon which we can build a knowledgeable, innovative, and conscious society. Contributing to educational initiatives, be it through mentoring, tutoring, or supporting organizations that make education accessible, is an enormous way to affect positive change. When we elevate the minds around us, we see our communities and, ultimately, our world thrive.

Advocacy and activism can be potent ways to fulfill our social responsibility. Joining movements that align with your values, championing causes you're passionate about, and being a vocal and active participant in societal change is vital. Use your voice, your platform, and your network to shed light on issues that matter. Ignite discussions, spur actions, and drive the momentum of progress.

Looking closer at the grand picture, promoting health and well-being beyond personal fitness is part of our collective responsibility. Back initiatives that push for better healthcare systems, mental health awareness, and accessible fitness facilities for underprivileged communities. When one of us is better off, it has a positive knock-on effect on the entire community.

Remember to lead with empathy and kindness in every interaction. The way we treat those around us—our colleagues, employees, and community members—reflects our integrity and respect for humanity. Kindness can transform lives and impart a sense of belonging and care, which in turn creates a nurturing environment for everyone to flourish.

Lastly, measure success not just in material gains or personal accolades, but also in terms of the positive impact you've had on the world and the lives you've touched. It's in the balance of individual pursuits with social contributions that we find a deeper fulfillment and a lasting legacy.

So, weave social responsibility into your fabric of excellence. Let it be the golden thread that adds richness and texture to your tapestry of achievements. After all, your true power lies not just in what you become, but in what you give back. Make your mark; create a ripple that will turn into waves of change and upliftment for others as you continue your champion's journey.

Chapter 24

Preparing for the Future

As we pivot from the ethical scaffolding that undergirds our path to victory, our gaze must now shift toward the horizon—toward preparing for the future, which demands a blend of anticipation and strategic agility. Picture the future as a canvas, where the paint hasn't dried yet; it's a work in progress, shaped by your present actions and the plans you lay down. Crafting a future that resonates with your aspirations involves recognizing potential challenges before they emerge, allowing you to navigate around them deftly or meet them head-on with resilience. It's about adopting a mindset that sees beyond immediate triumphs, keeping your long-term vision crystal clear in your sights. By infusing your strategies with readiness for change, versatility in approach, and an unshakable commitment to your ultimate goals, you'll find yourself not just walking into the future, but actively shaping it to your contour. In this future, your legacy as a winner is not left to chance, but carefully constructed with intention and thoughtful foresight.

Anticipating Challenges

As you've charted your course to victory and embraced the pursuit of your full potential, it's crucial to recognize the bumps and hurdles that will inevitably dot your path. In this section, we're not just glossing over the potential difficulties; we're facing them head-on. It's preparatory work, an invaluable part of the process that fortifies us against the unpredictability of life's trials.

Firstly, understand that challenges aren't roadblocks; they're the stepping stones to your growth. When setting out on a journey of self-improvement, it's tempting to dream of smooth sailing, but the truth is, that growth often comes from discomfort. Whether it's a missed deadline, a negative performance review, or a personal setback, each challenge bears seeds of learning and resilience. Embrace them, turn them over in your hands, and pick out the lessons they offer.

Expect to encounter self-doubt. Even the most confident among us can be rattled by the inner critic that questions our choices and whispers of possible failure. While it's natural to experience these moments, what sets champions apart is their ability to engage in constructive self-dialogue. Replace the whispers of doubt with reaffirming thoughts that underscore your ability and your journey's worth.

Resistance from your environment, too, is a challenge to anticipate. Not every friend, family member, or colleague will understand or support your transformation. It can be disheartening when the encouragement you crave isn't forthcoming, but remember, you're not doing this for them. Remain steadfast in your focus, seek out like-minded individuals, and build a community that aligns with your goals.

Financial constraints can present a formidable challenge. When aiming for growth in any aspect of life, finances often play a critical role. Whether it's further education, a business venture, or personal development programs, these are investments in your future. Pre-plan and budget wisely, but also keep an eye out for resources that can help you advance without breaking the bank.

Time management will test you. With just 24 hours in a day, fitting in all that you wish to achieve can seem daunting. This is where your ability to prioritize comes into play. Accept that you can't do everything at once. It's about making strategic compromises and being disciplined in how you allocate your time to what truly matters.

Physical and mental health setbacks are also part of life. Your body and mind are your primary tools; when they're not at peak performance, neither are you. Anticipate fluctuations in your health by establishing routines that maintain and nourish your well-being. And if challenges arise, adapt accordingly—rest if necessary but remain committed to your overall goal.

Sometimes the challenges will be intangible, like a sudden loss of motivation. On those days when the fire seems to have dwindled, revisit your 'why.' Recalling your deeper purpose can rekindle the energy needed to forge ahead. Create a motivational toolbox – encompassing your vision board, affirmations, and success stories – ready to fuel your drive whenever it wanes.

Change is another constant you'll face. Markets fluctuate, trends evolve, and life itself can turn on a dime. Your ability to anticipate and adapt to change is a mark of a true champion. It requires you to stay informed, flexible, and open to pivoting your strategies. Cultivate a mindset that sees change not as a threat but as an opportunity for innovation and improvement.

Moreover, preparing for unexpected opportunities is just as important. Luck favors the prepared, and sometimes, it's the opportunities you haven't planned for that can lead to breakthrough success. Keep a keen eye on the horizon for the chance encounters or offers that align with your goals and be ready to seize them with both hands.

Emotional highs and lows will accompany you like shadows throughout your journey. Riding the wave of emotions is part of being human. The key is not to let your feelings dictate your actions. Acknowledge them, certainly, but base your decisions on your values and the strategies you've laid out for yourself.

What happens when you hit a plateau, where growth seems to have stalled? This too, is a challenge that many face. Keep reassessing your approach, stay curious, and be willing to experiment. Sometimes, a slight tweak in your methods or adopting a new perspective can reignite progress.

External criticism is also an inevitable part of pushing the boundaries. Not every piece of feedback will be affirming or gently delivered. Learn to filter criticism constructively – taking on board what is helpful and disregarding what is not – without it diminishing your sense of self or your determination to succeed.

At times, commitment to your goals will clash with other life responsibilities, whether that's family, relationships, or other duties. This balancing act is delicate and requires constant vigilance and adjustment. Keep communication channels open with those around you and be transparent about your ambitions and the constraints they may impose.

Lastly, navigating ethical dilemmas and maintaining integrity can be challenging amidst intense competition or the pressure to succeed at any cost.

Define your red lines early on and commit to upholding them. Winning is hollow if it isn't achieved with honor.

Anticipating challenges allows you to create a game plan, ensuring that when you do encounter them, you're not blindsided. Instead, you'll approach them with the same assuredness and strategic thinking that champions apply to their entire journey. Each challenge is an invitation to problem-solving, to learning, and to strengthening your path to sustainable success. Rise to meet them, knowing they are integral markers of your growth and your enduring legacy as a winner.

Strategic Planning and Readiness

Strategic Planning and Readiness is the cerebral architecture of your success roadmap. It's plotting your course with intention and foresight. Remember, a ship without a rudder is at the mercy of the sea—just as a dreamer without a plan can be tossed about by life's unpredictable currents. But equipped with strategic planning, you're setting your sails towards the horizon with determination and readiness to adjust to whatever winds may come your way.

Think of strategic planning as your personal game of chess against the grandmaster called life. It's about knowing your moves, predicting possible outcomes, and staying flexible enough to adapt as the game unfolds. Every champion understands that victory doesn't just happen; it's orchestrated through a meticulous blueprint—one where you're both the architect and the builder.

Now, let's talk readiness. It's not merely a state of preparedness; it encapsulates a proactive mindset. You've got to train your senses to sniff out opportunity and your reflexes to embrace change. It's about honing that anticipation reflex, so when the door of opportunity swings open, you're the first one stepping through.

To be strategically savvy, begin with asking the big-picture questions. Where are you heading? Why does it matter? What will it take to get there? This goes beyond setting goals—it's about setting the right goals. Goals that aren't just sparks but torchbearers illuminating your path. Such clarity doesn't jumble your thoughts; instead, it jettisons confusion and crystallizes focus.

Construct a plan that's robust yet flexible; think of it as a trellis that guides and supports, but also allows for growth in new directions. Life thrives on change, and your strategies should be no different. Circumstances evolve, and your plan must be alive and breathing, able to evolve too.

Meticulously dissect your end goal into bite-sized pieces. Like a puzzle, every piece is essential, and while each may be a small part of the bigger picture, it's the strategic placement of these that creates the masterpiece. And remember, the brightest roadmaps have room for improvisation—sometimes the best routes aren't found on the map; they're discovered along the journey.

Your strategic plan is also your commitment device. It's you declaring to yourself and the universe that you're serious—boldly willing to work through the sweat, the setbacks, and the soreness. It's understanding that readiness is not about assuming a perfect journey. It's about being unshakably willing to face the imperfect and turning it to your advantage.

Let's pivot to the tools of readiness. Yes, you've got your intrinsic talents, but what's the arsenal you're building to conquer your quests? Knowledge, skills, networks, and resources—these are your allies in ensuring readiness for the battleground of success. Build relationships that broaden your strategy, and invest in skills that sharpen your edge. Each asset you acquire is another notch in your belt of readiness.

Don't just prepare for the expected; be ready for its antithesis. The curveballs, the outlier events, the black swan moments—they're not just possibilities; they're eventualities waiting to test your resilience. Strategic readiness isn't just about having a Plan B; it's about having a full alphabet of contingencies.

Forethought is your foresight's muscle. Flex it. Stretch it with scenarios and simulations. What if funding fails? What if technology shifts? What if your dream team member decides to leave? Thinking through these now prevents being blindsided later. This is not about harboring fear—it's about empowering yourself with proactive confidence.

Growth and comfort can't ride the same bike; if you want to grow, comfort needs to hop off. Readiness demands stepping out of your comfort zone, pushing limits, and consistently recalibrating your efforts. It's a dynamic state—a spirited dance between the planned and the spontaneous.

In your pursuit of greatness, remember that your most valuable player is adaptability. It's the resilience to pivot, the agility to leap towards opportunity, and the skill to navigate through storms. Strategic planning imbued with adaptability is a combo that's tough to beat.

Much like the riggings and ropes that brace a mast, your core values guide your strategic plan. They're the moral compass that guides decisions, actions, and course corrections. When you align your plan with your values, you'll find a congruence that keeps internal conflict at bay and integrity as your constant companion.

Finally, celebrate the milestones, both big and small. The joy of your journey lies not just in your destination but in each stride towards it. Strategic planning and readiness include recognizing when it's time to raise a glass to a win or to learn from a challenge. It's a harmonious balance of striving forward while being firmly grounded in each new moment.

As you arm yourself with strategy and readiness, you're not just preparing to fight battles; you're setting up to win wars. And in the grand campaign of your ambitions, remember that the war won is not just about achieving goals, but about conquering oneself. With every strategic step, you're tearing down old barriers and building a fortress of potential, fortified by your willingness to plan, adapt, and be ready for the greatness you've set out to achieve.

Conclusion

Your Champion's Journey Continues

The road that twists and turns under your feet, the journey of personal triumph and collective victory doesn't end on the last page of this narrative. Rather, it casts its gaze forward, beckoning you to tread ever onward to horizons yet unseen. As you've equipped yourself with a quiver of tools, insights, and strategies throughout this book, remember that the true test is in their application in the living, breathing theater of your life.

We've woven through the fabric of visionary goals, the resilience found in the heart of a champion, and the iron-clad discipline that undergirds achievement. Alongside these conceptual titans, motivation has been both the spark and the fuel. With every chapter turned, you've been assembling an inner fortress capable of overcoming fear and doubt, learning to dance with failure and court success with a smile.

The increments of daily growth are sometimes imperceptible, yet they accumulate into a staggering ascent. Your routine, etched into the bedrock of your every day, rises not as a wall but as a ladder, each rung a step towards the zenith of your full potential. Remain conscious of this. Positivity and gratitude weave the safety net that will catch you should you stumble, ensuring that even a fall shapes itself into a learning curve.

As you map out the minutes and hours of your days, prioritize. Time is a currency that admits no refunds, and procrastination is akin to squandering your wealth. Invest, instead, in relationships that bolster your ascent, in conversations that challenge and grow your capacity to communicate with eloquence and to listen with intent.

The temple that houses your spirit requires care. Nutrition and fitness are not add-ons but essentials, fueling a body that can carry the dreams of a mind in demand. Balance isn't just a concept for gymnasts; it's a principle for life. Let 'no' be a word that serves you, allowing focus in a sea of distractions.

Financial foresight and the courage to engage in the give-and-take of negotiation imbue your actions with the sagacity required for sustained success. Leadership is more than a title; it's an action, a responsibility to ignite the potential in others. As you develop, be the spark that lights a thousand other flames—it's a fire that will perpetually warm you back.

Innovation keeps you at the cutting edge, a step ahead, and continually creative in a world that never stops changing. Technology is a tool—use it to carve a niche that is undeniably yours, broadcasting your brand to a world waiting to hear what you have to say.

Learning doesn't cease with a degree or a title; it's an enduring pursuit. Diversify your sources, seek wisdom in unusual places, and never assume you've heard it all. Mindfulness is not just a buzzword; it's the foundation of presence, the art of immersing yourself so fully in the now that each moment becomes a profound experience.

Travel, with its rich tapestry of cultures and insights, is more than mere escapism. It's an investment into the breadth of your understanding and the depth of your empathy. Each new landscape is a conversation with a broader version of you, an expansion that refuses to be reined in.

Let victory be acknowledged and celebrated—let your milestones be markers of remembrance and occasions for joy. But also tolerate criticism and feedback. Learn to sift the wheat from the chaff, capturing the essentials from every voice that seeks to shape your path.

Sustainability is about vision: a planet-conscious approach that values not just the ends but the means of your accomplishments. And integrity, the ethics of your endeavor, demands that you play fair even when no one's watching. It's the invisible crown of honor that shines the brightest.

Preparing for the future isn't about crystal balls and prophecy—it's about agility, readiness to pivot, and an understanding that what lies ahead may require of you not just to walk but sometimes to sprint, other times to pause and take stock. Always, always towards growth. Always towards the light of undiscovered potential.

This isn't the end; it's a pause. Take a breath. Reflect. Now step forward, your shoes filled with the certainty of your past learnings, and stride into the boundlessness of your tomorrows. The epilogue of this part of your story is just the prologue to the next.

Your champion's journey continues, not because there are more pages to be read, but because there is more life to be led. Set your sights not just on your next goal, but on the constellation of possibilities that is your life escape. With each new sunrise, you are invited to begin again, to chase the horizon with vigor and an open heart.

And so, as this book closes, your grandest chapter yet beckons. The journey continues—it's yours to define. Choose boldly, live passionately, and never doubt that within you beats the heart of a champion.

Printed in the USA
CPSIA information can be obtained
at www.ICGtesting.com
CBHW072355020724
11065CB00015B/657

9 798869 059840